Time and Space

A Basic Reader

MICHAEL CONNELLY
and
JEAN SIMS

PRENTICE HALL REGENTS, Upper Saddle River, NJ 07458

Library of Congress Cataloging-in-Publication Data

Connelly, Michael.
  Time and space, a basic reader/Michael Connelly & Jean Sims.
—2nd ed.

  Rev. ed. of: Time and space, a basic reader, ©1982.
  Bibliography
  ISBN 0-13-922014-3
  1. English language—Textbooks for foreign speakers.
  2. Readers—1950– I. Sims, Jean. II. Connelly, Michael. Time and
space, a basic reader. III. Title
  [PE1128.C694   1989]
  428.6′4—dc20   89–33552
                                                        CIP

Editorial/production supervision: *Janet Johnston*
Interior design: *Ed Lee*
Cover design: *20/20 Services, Inc.*
Cover illustration: The Image Bank
                    Photo by *John Wagner, Jr.*
Manufacturing buyer: *Ray Keating*

20   19   18   17   16   15   14   13

ISBN 0-13-922014-3

Prentice-Hall International (UK) Limited, *London*
Prentice-Hall of Australia Pty. Limited, *Sydney*
Prentice-Hall Canada Inc., *Toronto*
Prentice-Hall Hispanoamericana, S.A., *Mexico*
Prentice-Hall of India Private Limited, *New Delhi*
Prentice-Hall of Japan, Inc., *Tokyo*
Pearson Education Asia Pte. Ltd., *Singapore*
Editora Prentice-Hall do Brasil, Ltda., *Rio de Janeiro*

Contents

Acknowledgments

We want to thank Mr. Bill Ginevicz of Boulder, Colorado, who did the drawings for this book. We appreciate the help of Ms. Pat Wilcox Peterson, who read our materials, made many helpful suggestions, and offered support and encouragement. Our thanks also to Bill Sims, who generously loaned us photographic equipment, and to our families, who sacrificed their time with us.

Photo Credits

The authors acknowledge with thanks the help of the following individuals and organizations.

Figure	
1–3	National Aeronautics and Space Administration
16	National Park Service, Great Sand Dunes National Monument, Colorado
17	University of Colorado Museum, Boulder, Colorado
18	Denver Museum of Natural History, Denver, Colorado
22	The British Museum, London, England
24	National Bureau of Standards, U.S. Department of Commerce, Boulder, Colorado
26, 27, 29, 50	National Oceanic and Atmospheric Administration, Boulder, Colorado
28	KOA-TV, Channel 4, Denver, Colorado
35, 36, 49	Museum of Science and Industry, Chicago, Illinois
39	Phil Stietenroth, Biomedical Communications, University of Colorado Health Services Center, Denver, Colorado
41	The University of Texas at Austin News and Information Service
46	National Center for Atmospheric Research, Boulder, Colorado
52	National Park Service, Flagstaff, Arizona

Introduction

In the past ten years, there has been a great deal of research into how reading actually takes place, and the field of teaching reading has changed dramatically. At present, reading is generally viewed as an *interactive process.* This process is not just a matter of the reader getting information from a text; rather, the information from the text interacts with the knowledge already stored in the reader's memory (*schemata*). The schemata are continually modified, expanded, and refined in the interaction occurring between reader and text.

The reader handles the incoming information by two methods: bottom-up processing (decoding incoming data) and top-down processing (higher level concepts); both methods are available to the reader at the same time. It is generally accepted that both bottom-up and top-down processing skills are basic to good reading and that there is interaction among the levels. Therefore, both strategies must be developed.

From research in how reading takes place, can we determine the best way to spend the time in the reading class?

First, we agree with Eskey and Grabe, who said, "Both top-down and bottom-up skills can, in the long run, only be developed by extensive reading over time. Classroom work can point the way but cannot substitute for the act itself: people learn to read by reading, not by doing exercises."[1]

Time and Space contains many readings on adult topics from a variety of academic disciplines, with a major emphasis on scientific and technological topics. Each chapter contains a cluster of two or three readings on a related topic, with each successive reading in the chapter increasing in difficulty. The readings are written in simple English and are controlled both lexically and syntactically so that upper-beginning to low-intermediate readers can read them easily and quickly.

Topics have been chosen because (a) they are of high interest to adults; (b) students may have already studied these subjects in their own languages and, therefore, have available schemata that can be utilized; and (c) the topics utilize the concept of narrow reading recommended by Krashen.

Narrow reading—reading on a single topic or reading the texts of a single author—is more efficient for second language reading. "In narrow reading, the text becomes easier to comprehend after the first few pages. Readers adjust to repeated vocabulary of a particular topic and/or the particular style of a writer. Repetitions of vocabulary and structure mean that review is built into the reading. Schemata are repeatedly accessed and further expanded and refined, resulting in increased comprehension."[2]

Since we believe that people learn to read by reading and not by doing exercises, we gave careful thought to the kinds of exercises to include in this book. As Rigg says:

We are not helping them [students] become good readers by treating reading as an exact process requiring three people—author, reader, and teacher. It is easy to confuse reading with reading instruction, but the two are separate processes and should be treated so. Reading is what the student does alone, with the text. Reading instruction is what the teacher does with the students to help them when they read. . . . Allowing the reader to read without interfering . . . lets the reader develop and use the strategies of prediction, confirmation, and correction, strategies which can be developed only through reading.[3]

In addition to reading, what kind of classroom instruction will best help the student develop efficient reading strategies? Mark Clarke concludes that

behaviors which are most productively and effectively taught are:

1. Concentration on passage-level semantic cues.

2. Formulation of hypotheses about the text before reading, then reading to confirm, refine or reject hypotheses.

3. Deemphasis of graphophonic and syntactic accuracy, that is, a tolerance for inexactness, a willingness to take chances and make mistakes.[4]

For practice in these behaviors, we created four categories of exercises (introductory exercises, reading for meaning exercises, reading faster exercises, and vocabulary exercises) that emphasize a willingness to take chances and make mistakes. Each exercise is intended to be an integral part of the process of making a hypothesis, reading to confirm or reject the hypothesis, reading quickly for meaning, guessing the meaning of new words and, finally, checking to confirm understanding of the reading.

1. *Introductory Exercises.* Introductory discussion questions, pictures and games activate the reader's schemata and introduce vocabulary.

First, introductory discussion questions set the scene and ask readers to form a hypothesis about what they will read. The many photographs, drawings, diagrams, maps, and graphs in each chapter also provide discussion material for the teacher and students before reading. Studies have shown that "the use of pictures in making predictions and activating schemata has a greater effect on beginning and intermediate students than other types of treatment."[5] Teachers should use new vocabulary in discussing the introductory questions and talking about the pictures but should not teach vocabulary as such at this point.

The optional games and/or activities located in the Discussion Activities can be used by the teacher to introduce the chapter or as a concluding activity. Particularly effective examples for introduction are (a) visual aids, such as maps, vacation pictures, postcards, stamps, and money that students can bring to talk about and pass around the class, and (b) activities such as watching TV weather reports, trying to draw a map or a symbol, locating geographical points on a world map, taking a trip to the Post Office, playing the memory game, and trying left brain and right brain activities before reading. These build enthusiasm, activate schemata, and introduce vocabulary in context.

2. *Reading for Meaning Exercises.* According to Joanne Devine,

> Students bring their theoretical orientations to the second language reading process. Their orientations may influence how much their low English ability restricts second language reading ability and their ability to effectively combine top-down and bottom-up strategies. [It has been shown that] a meaning-centered approach may mitigate the effects of low general language proficiency, thus allowing the reader to transfer first language reading strategies to the second language.[6]

In each chapter we have created three types of exercises that provide practice in reading for meaning:

- *Comprehension Exercises* include both literal and inferential comprehension questions. Inferential comprehension questions encourage reading for meaning.
- Exercises in *Reading to Find the Main Idea.* Students are given three titles from which to choose the main idea of a paragraph. Since students are to discriminate between the titles, they may need some instruction about topic sentences and supporting ideas. As practice, students can go back to any already completed reading to underline the main ideas and then compare their choices as a class activity.
- In *Using the Context* exercises, students are given a paragraph that includes some blanks. They are asked to read the paragraph and answer a true/false question. This demonstrates that they can understand the main idea of the paragraph even though they do not understand every word. It also encourages "a tolerance for inexactness and a willingness to take chances and make mistakes."[7] Then, students are asked to fill in the blanks from a list of words or, in later chapters, to fill in the blanks without a supplied word list.

3. *Reading Faster Exercises.* A recurrent goal throughout all the exercises in this book is increased reading speed. Speed may be the most important element in reading for meaning.

> The teacher must induce students to abandon the word-by-word approach to reading by introducing exercises, like timed readings, which force the students to read faster, and exercises that, for similar reasons, force students to read in meaningful 'chunks.' The major bottom-up skill that readers of a second language must acquire is the skill of reading as fast in that language as their knowledge of it will allow them to, in relation to their reading purposes. Specific rates must, of course, be adjusted to the reader's purpose in reading a particular text (along a spectrum that runs from skimming for the main idea to close reading for an upcoming exam) but the principal holds, and doing any kind of reading at much less than 200 words a minute is certain to affect comprehension adversely.[8]

A skimming exercise, Reading to Find the Main Idea (previously discussed), and a scanning exercise, Reading to Find Information, are included in each chapter. In Reading to Find Information, students are asked to read a question and to find and underline the answer as quickly as possible in the paragraph that follows. Teachers should encourage speed. It is not necessary to read every word in the paragraph.

A timed reading in each chapter is meant to be read twice, and supplemental readings in half the chapters are also set up as timed readings. The teacher should time these readings and have students chart their progress on the charts located in the back of this book. This concrete evidence of their reading speed progress is motivating and fun.

We recommend rereading the timed readings. Teachers are usually concerned that repeated readings will lead to boredom, but students are usually excited by the gains they make in fluency. To help students understand why they are rereading, teachers should lead them in a discussion of how athletes and musicians spend hours practicing basic skills until they develop speed and facility. Repeated readings provide this same type of practice. Comprehension may be poor on the first reading of the text, but with each additional rereading, the student will be better able to overcome the decoding barrier to comprehension. Rereading builds both fluency and comprehension.[9]

4. *Vocabulary.* The 1,000-word frequency sources were Kucera and Francis, *A Computational Analysis of Present Day American English,* and West, *The General Service List.* Words in the readings that are not on the 1,000-word lists are either defined in the text, glossed at the bottom of the pages, or identifiable in accompanying pictures. Students are asked to read quickly and to guess at the meaning of new words. This gives students the opportunity to attack new words in context and helps them develop a willingness to take chances. Even at a low level, it develops the good habit of reading until the meaning of the word starts to become clear from the context of the developing discourse.

Readings have been constructed so that new vocabulary appears a number of times in different contexts throughout the book. General academic vocabulary is used again and again in succeeding chapters There is a great deal of interrelation of vocabulary between chapters. Vocabulary is also expanded within chapters. The first reading is rather simple; the second builds on vocabulary in the first; the third (supplemental reading) builds on vocabulary in the first two and expands even more.

Finally, two crossword puzzles and two word family vocabulary exercises give students the opportunity to play with the vocabulary they have already learned in context. These exercises are introduced *after* the chapters in which the words first appear and should serve as reinforcement.

5. *Whole-Group and Small-Group Discussion and Application of Words and Ideas.* At the end of each chapter, students should be given an opportunity to use the new vocabulary and new ideas they have encountered and to try to relate them to their own ideas or opinions. To achieve this, in each chapter there are:

- *Discussion Activities*. Some items in this category are appropriate for introduction and have previously been discussed. Other discussion items are best used as concluding discussion activities, either in whole-group discussion or small-group discussion groups, after which students report back to the whole class on the results of their discussions. The teacher should determine which discussion activity is most appropriate for each individual class.
- *Timed Reading Comprehension Check*. Five true/false or multiple choice questions are included but are not intended as a test. Rather, the exercise includes inferential, personal opinion, and even some controversial questions. The class can be divided into small groups to discuss the answers. If students in the small groups do not agree on the answers, encourage them to arrive at a consensus. A vocabulary exercise is also provided at the end of each chapter. It uses vocabulary from the chapter in a new context to help determine if the students really understand the meaning of the vocabulary words.

Structures used in the readings include the following:

Verb Forms

		Modals	
present	past	can, can't	could
present continuous	future	must	may
present perfect (where		will	might
necessary for authenticity)		would	

(Appendix 2 gives additional explanation of modals)

Connectors

		Wh-Questions		
and	but	who	where	how
or	so that	what	why	how many
as	before	when	which	how much
however	because			

Yes/no questions			Infinitives: (verb + to + verb)	
Here/there			Conditionals (real)	
There is/there are			Comparisons:	
Pronouns			same, different, -er than	
Determiners:			more/less than, as . . . as	
the	some	this	all	the most, -est
a	any	that	both	Adverbs: -ly, very, too
an	all	these	each	Cardinal and ordinal numbers
	other	those	another	(Appendix 1 gives an additional ex-

Possessive nouns and pronouns
planation and practices with

Reflexive pronouns
numbers)

Prepositional phrases
Days, dates, months

Passives (only a few examples where
Clauses: that, who, which, and when

necessary for authenticity)
clauses when the referent is clear

Notes

1. David Eskey and William Grabe, "Interactive Models for Second Language Reading: Perspectives on Instruction," *Interactive Approaches to Teaching Reading* (New York: Cambridge University Press, 1988).

2. Stephen Krashen, *Principles and Practice in Second Language Acquisition* (New York: Pergamon, 1982).

3. Pat Rigg, "On TESOL 77: Teaching and Learning ESL: Trends in Research and Practice" (Washington, D.C.: TESOL, 1977).

4. Mark Clarke, "The Short Circuit Hypothesis of ESL Reading or When Language Competence Interferes With Reading Performance," *Modern Language Journal* 64 (2): 203–209.

5. Thom Hudson, "Effects of Induced Schemata on the Short Circuit in L2 Reading: Non-decoding Factors in L2 Reading and Performance," *Language Learning* 32 (1): 3–31.

6. Joanne Devine, "A Case Study of Two Readers: Models of Reading and Reading Performance," *Interactive Approaches to Teaching Reading,* eds. Carroll, Devine & Eskey (New York: Cambridge University Press, 1988).

7. Clarke, "Short Circuit Hypothesis."

8. Eskey and Grabe, "Interactive Models."

9. Jay Samuels, "The Method of Repeated Readings," *The Reading Teacher,* 1979.

chapter 1 _____

The Moon

Introduction

Directions: *Talk about these questions before you read the story.*

What do you know about the moon?
Is it near or far from us?
Is it like the earth?
Do people live there?
Have people visited there?

Directions: *Read the story quickly. Try to guess the meaning of new words. Don't use your dictionary.*

When people look up into the sky, they can see that it is not empty. During the day, they can see the sun. At night, they see the moon and many, many stars. Scientists want to learn more about the sun and the moon because they are near us. The stars are very far away, so people can't go there yet. However, people have already been on the moon. Scientists know a lot about it.

The moon is nearer than the sun. The moon is about 240,000 miles away. The sun is farther, 93 million miles from us. When people look at the moon, it looks almost as large as the sun. That is because it is much nearer. The sun is really much larger.

The sun is a star. It is a ball of fire; it sends out light. The moon is rocky and hard. It is not hot. It does not send out light; it reflects light. This means that the moon does not make its own light. The sun sends out light to the moon. Then the moon sends the sun's light back to the earth.

The moon is very different from the earth. There is no air on the moon. It is both very hot and very cold there. During the day, it is very hot in the sunshine, but at night it can be − 200°F. (129° below zero C.).

There are no trees, grass, or water on the moon, only rocks and deserts. There are many mountains that are from 2 to 5 miles high. There are at least 30,000 round holes in the moon called craters. Some of the craters are half a mile wide, but some are as large as 160 miles wide.

A moon is a smaller object in space that goes around a planet. Our moon goes around our earth. It takes about 28 days for the moon to go around the earth. At the same time, the moon itself also turns. This takes about 28 days too. This is why one side of the moon is always turned toward the earth. The other side is always turned away. Spaceships went around the moon in the 1960s. They took the first pictures of the back side of the moon.

In July 1969, two men from the United States stepped on the moon. They took some machines to make some tests. They brought back 48 pounds of rocks from the moon.

Figure 1   The moon

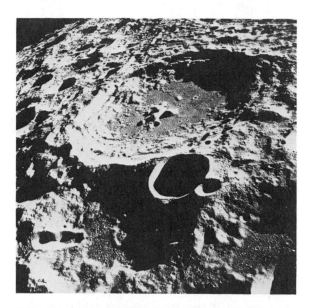

Figure 2 The back side of the moon with craters

Scientists have learned many things from that trip to the moon. They have learned that the rocks are 3.5 billion years old. They are not like rocks on the earth. There are many things about the moon that scientists still do not know.

The first trip to the moon was very important. It means that now human beings have walked on a place different from the earth. It is a beginning. It is a step to all the other planets and stars.

Check Your Guess

Directions: *You guessed the meaning of these words from this story. Circle the letter beside the answer that gives the same idea as the new word. Do not use your dictionary.*

1. When we look up into the sky, we can see that is is not <u>empty</u>. During the day, we can see the sun. At night, we see the moon and many, many stars.
   a. There are many things in it.
   b. There is nothing in it.
   c. There are a few things in it.

2. <u>Scientists</u> want to learn more about the sun and the moon because they are near us.
   a. people who study science
   b. people who write books
   c. people who teach in universities

3. The moon does not send out light; it <u>reflects</u> light. This means that the moon does not make its own light.
   a. makes light
   b. sends back light from another place
   c. shines

4. There are round holes in the moon called <u>craters</u>. There are at least 30,000 craters on the moon.
   a. mountains
   b. rivers
   c. holes

5. <u>Spaceships</u> went around the moon in the 1960s.
   a. boats that go on the sea
   b. airplanes that fly above the earth
   c. machines that take people off the earth into space

6. It was a step to all the other <u>planets</u> and stars.
   a. An example of a planet is the sun.
   b. An example of a planet is the moon.
   c. An example of a planet is the earth.

Comprehension Exercises

Part 1: *You can find the answers to these questions in the story. You may look back to find an answer if you don't remember.*

1. Is the moon as large as the sun?

2. How is the moon different from the sun?

3. How far from the moon is the earth? How far is it from the sun?

4. How is the moon different from the earth?

5. Two men walked on the moon in 1969. What country were they from? Do you know their names?

6. What did scientists learn about the moon from that trip?

Part 2: *You may not find the answers to these questions in the story, but you can answer the questions if you understand the ideas.*

1. Stars make their own light; planets and moons reflect light. Is the sun a star or a planet? Is the earth a star or a planet?

2. Do you think anything can live on the moon? Why or why not?

3. Why can't we see one side of the moon?

Comprehension Check

Directions: *Read each sentence. Write T if it is true. Write F if it is false. Do not look back in the story.*

_____ 1. The sun is nearer to us than the moon.

_____ 2. The moon looks almost the same size as the sun.

_____ 3. The sun reflects light.

_____ 4. It is always very cold on the moon.

_____ 5. Some of the mountains on the moon are 5 miles high.

_____ 6. The largest of the craters on the moon are about half a mile wide.

_____ 7. We can see all of the moon.

_____ 8. The rocks on the moon are 3.5 billion years old.

_____ 9. The rocks from the moon are like rocks on earth.

_____ 10. The moon reflects light.

Discussion Activities

Directions: *Discuss these topics as a class or in a small group.*

1. Is it important for us to go to other planets and stars?

2. Draw a picture to explain this: The moon reflects the sun's light.

3. Do you want to go to the moon in a spaceship? Why or why not?

4. Plan a trip to the moon in the year 3003. You are going there to live. You are not coming back. What do you want to take with you? Talk about work, clothes, family, photographs, anything that is important to you.

Is There Life in Space?

Directions: *Read quickly. Your teacher will time you. Put your reading rate on Chart 1 in the back of this book.*

On a clear night you can see many stars in the sky. These stars	14
are millions of miles away. Scientists want to know what the stars are	27
like. Are they balls of fire? Do they have large rocks or sand, like our	42
moon? There is another question they want to know much more about.	54
Are there living things on any of the stars?	63

People have always thought about this question. It was not	73
possible to find the answer before now. Now scientists know more	84
about space than ever before. Now they have some machines that can	96
help them look for the answer.	102

How will scientists do this? People can't go to the stars. The	114
stars are much too far away. It would take hundreds of years for a	128
person to go to the next star in a spaceship. So scientists are sending out	143
radio signals.*	145

These signals go through space at the speed of light, almost 6	157
trillion miles in a year. At that speed, it will take 25 years for radio	172
signals to reach the next star. The signals ask, "Is anyone out there?"	185
Living things in space must have machines to hear the signals. We will	198
not get an answer to our signals for more than 50 years, but scientists are	213
already listening. They think someone from space may be trying to send	225
signals to us.	228

Scientists also have sent large telescopes into space. A	237
telescope is a machine that makes things look larger. When you look into	250
it, things that are far away look nearer. The telescopes are going around	263
the earth. They are looking out into space. They are looking for life in	277
other worlds.	279

Maybe in the next few years we will get an answer to the	292
question "Is there life in space?"	298

*signal–information sent by radio

READING SKILLS EXERCISES

Reading to Find Information

Directions: *Read the question. Then move your eyes over the paragraph that follows it. It is not necessary to read every word carefully. Just look for the answer to the question. Put a line under the answer. Work quickly.*

Is there life on the moon?

The rocks from the moon were very important. Scientists studied the rocks for a long time. They studied rocks from the mountains on the moon. They wanted to know if moon mountains were like earth mountains. They learned from moon rocks that there is no form of life on the moon.

Figure 3   A human walking on the moon for the first time

Was it easy to work in a space suit?

The space suits for the first men on the moon gave air to keep the men alive. It was very difficult for the men to move because the suits were very large and heavy. They had to stand up straight. They used a machine with a long handle to pick up rocks.

Will people live on the moon?

The moon is more than a light in the sky to us now. From the trips to the moon, scientists have more than 250 pounds of moon rocks, thousands of pictures, and much scientific information. We know what the moon is like. Now we do not think that people will live on the moon someday.

Timed Reading

Directions: *Read the timed reading again. Your teacher will time your reading. Put your reading rate on Chart 2 in the back of this book.*

Timed Reading Comprehension Check

Directions: 1. *Answer all the questions about the timed reading.*

2. *Go back to the timed reading and check your answers. Put a line under the answer in the timed reading. In the blank, write the line number where you found the answer in the timed reading.*

3. *When you have finished, your teacher may ask you to talk about the answers in a small group. In your group, try to agree on the answers and then report back to the class.*

Line
Number   Answer

_____   _____   1. Stars are made of
                                a. fire.
                                b. large rocks.
                                c. sand.
                                d. things we don't know.

_____   _____   2. Scientists can find out if there are living things in space by
                                a. going in a spaceship.
                                b. reading a book.
                                c. listening for radio signals.
                                d. answering the telephone.

                            True/False

_____   _____   3. If people on the stars do not have machines, we will not find out about them for a long time.

_____   _____   4. Radio signals can go faster than spaceships.

_____   _____   5. Scientists will not listen for radio signals until after 50 years.

Directions: *Choose one word from the list to put in each blank.*

empty   scientists
reflects   craters
spaceship   important
planets

1. _____ want to know what the stars are like.

2. It would take hundreds of years for a person to go to the next star in a _____.

3. Moon _____ do not have water in them; they are _____.

4. People can't go to the _____ now. They are too far away.

5. It may be _____ to know if there are other living things in space.

6. We can see ourselves in a mirror. The mirror _____ the way we look.

chapter 2 _____

Symbols

Introduction

Directions: *Talk about these questions before you read the story.*

Look at the pictures of symbols.

> Where have you seen pictures like these?
>
> Which of these symbols are used in your country?
>
> How can symbols help you?

Directions: *Read the story quickly. Try to guess the meaning of new words. Don't use your dictionary.*

A symbol is something that is used to show or represent something else. Numbers, letters of the alphabet, and words are all symbols. They are written symbols that show ideas.

The easiest symbols to understand are 0, 1, 2, 3, 4, 5, 6, 7, 8, and 9. We can put these 10 symbols together in different ways to make every possible number. All people on earth understand the ideas shown by these mathematical symbols. In fact, scientists think that if we ever meet living things from space, we will use mathematical symbols to try to talk to them.

Letters of the alphabet are symbols we can use to write a sound. We put letters together to make words. Words are symbols, too. For example, we want to write the idea of something that is living. It is made of wood, and it has leaves. We use the word *tree*. Other languages use different words or even different alphabets to make their symbol for *tree*.

The Egyptians made one of the earliest forms of writing called *hieroglyphics*. They used pictures to represent people and stories. We can still see examples of hieroglyphics in museums. They are very difficult for us to read.

ROAD SYMBOLS

HOTEL SYMBOLS

Figure 4   Road signs and hotel symbols

Europeans began to use picture symbols on road signs about 50 years ago. People speak many different languages in Europe, but they can drive in all European countries because of the picture symbols on the road signs.

In 1974, the U.S. Department of Transportation put these pictures together in a book, *Symbol Signs*. Now we find these pictures in most international airports, hotels, railroad stations, World's Fairs, Olympic Games, and any place where people speak many different languages. People travel all around the world, but they cannot speak all the languages. International travel is easier because of picture symbols.

Check Your Guess

Directions: *You guessed the meaning of these words from this story. Circle the letter beside the answer that gives the same idea as the new word.*

1. A symbol is something that is used to show or <u>represent</u> something else.
   a. find
   b. ask
   c. mean

2. We can put these 10 symbols together in different ways to make every <u>possible</u> number.
   a. all we can make
   b. many
   c. some

3. The Egyptians made one of the earliest forms of writing. They used pictures called <u>hieroglyphics.</u>
   a. writing in words with pictures
   b. writing in pictures, not words
   c. writing in words only

4. If we want to write the idea of something that is living, is made of wood, and has <u>leaves,</u> we can use the word tree.
   a. something not living
   b. something made of wood
   c. something on a tree

5. Letters of the <u>alphabet</u> are symbols we can use to write a sound.
   a. mail
   b. a, b, c, d, e, etc.
   c. idea

6. Now you can find these pictures in most international airports, hotels, railroad stations, <u>World's Fairs</u>, Olympic Games, and any place where people speak many different languages.

   a. a place where people are fair

   b. a place where people play games

   c. another place where international people are

7. The easiest symbols to understand are <u>0, 1, 2, 3, 4, 5, 6, 7, 8</u>, and <u>9</u>.

   a. picture symbols

   b. letters of the alphabet

   c. mathematical symbols

Comprehension Exercises

Part 1: *You can find the answers to these questions in the story. You may look back to find an answer if you don't remember.*

1. Give some examples of mathematical symbols.

2. Where can you find picture symbols?

3. In which book can you find many picture symbols?

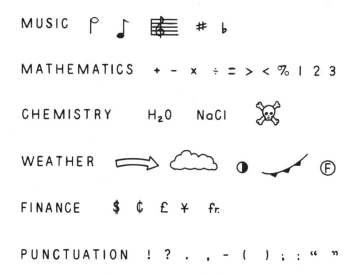

Figure 5   Common symbols

Figure 6 Match the words with the symbols.
Choose from the words below to fill the blanks:

Smoking	Restaurant	Bus	Information
No Smoking	Coffee Shop	Car Rental	Hotel Information
Men's Toilet	Gift Shop	Taxi	First Aid
Women's Toilet	Bar	Mail	Money Exchange
Baggage Claim	Elevator	Customs	Telephone

1. _____

2. _____

3. _____

4. _____

5. _____

6. _____

7. _____

8. _____

9. _____

10. _____

11. _____

12. _____

13. _____

14. _____

15. _____

16. _____

17. _____

18. _____

19. _____

20. _____

Part 2: *You may not find the answers to these questions in the story, but you can answer the questions if you understand the ideas.*

1. Why will we use mathematical symbols to try to talk to living things from space?

2. Why is Europe a good place to use picture symbols on signs?

3. How long do you think people have used symbols?

Comprehension Check

Directions: *Read each sentence. Write T if it is true. Write F if it is false. Do not look back in the story.*

_____ 1. A word is a written symbol of an idea.

_____ 2. Pictures are not symbols.

_____ 3. All people can understand the idea of mathematical symbols.

_____ 4. When we meet living things from space, we will use written words to talk to them.

_____ 5. There is only one alphabet in the world.

_____ 6. Picture symbols have been used for only about 50 years.

_____ 7. You must know two or three languages to be able to travel.

_____ 8. Picture symbols are used at the Olympic Games.

_____ 9. We need many symbols to make a lot of different numbers.

_____ 10. Many picture symbols are used by the Department of Transportation.

Discussion Activities

Directions: *Discuss these topics as a class or in a small group.*

1. Match the words to the pictures in Figure 6.

2. Look at the symbols in Figure 5. Can you guess what they mean?

3. Draw two or three new symbols. Can you make a funny symbol?

4. How can symbols help bring the people of the world closer together?

5. Which of the following symbols is the easiest to understand? Which is the most difficult? Why?

    letters, words, numbers, pictures

6. Using pictures only, write a letter to people in space.

Pioneer 10

Directions: *Read quickly. Your teacher will time you. Put your reading rate on Chart 1 in the back of this book.*

In 1972, scientists sent Pioneer 10, a spaceship, into space. It	11
went by Mars and Jupiter and took pictures. Then it went to the end of	26
the solar system. In 1983, Pioneer 10 became the first thing made by	39
humans to leave the solar system. It is still flying. It is traveling 30,558	53
miles an hour. It is still sending back information to scientists.	64

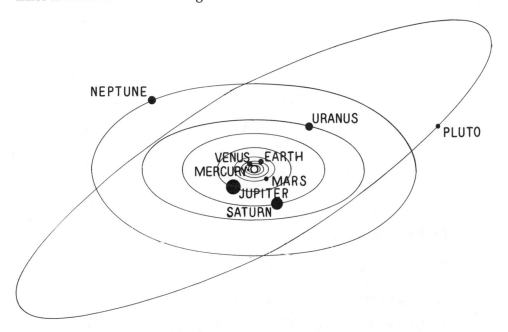

Figure 7   The solar system

Pioneer 10 has information in symbols on it. The information	74
is like a letter to a friend. It is for living things outside our solar system.	90
Maybe they will see the letter on Pioneer 10. In picture symbols, the	103
letter tells the answers to these questions:	110
Who are we?	113
What do we look like?	118
Where are we in the solar system?	125
Why did we send Pioneer 10?	131

Scientists think Pioneer 10 will never stop flying. It will fly   142
near another star in the year 34,590. Then it will fly near another star   156
every million years after that. Maybe other living things will find it.   168
When they see the picture symbols, maybe they will come to find us.   181

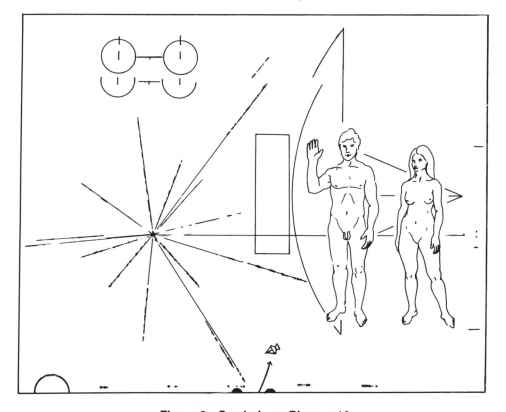

Figure 8   Symbols on Pioneer 10

READING SKILLS EXERCISES

Reading to Find Information

Directions: *Read the question. Then move your eyes over the paragraph that follows it. It is not necessary to read every word carefully. Just look for the answer to the question. Put a line under the answer. Work quickly.*

Why are picture symbols on road signs?

You can drive in another country. You can read road signs. You don't have to know how to read another language. The road signs are symbols. When you drive, you must look at the road signs quickly. Sometimes you need to read the road signs in bad weather. Road signs must be easy to see and understand.

Reading to Find the Main Idea

Directions: *Read the three titles. Then read the paragraph. Choose the title that is best for the whole paragraph.*

    a. Language Problems in an International Airport
    b. Picture Symbols in an International Airport
    c. How to Find the Bathroom in an International Airport

In an international airport, planes bring people from all countries. They speak many different languages and they are all in a hurry. They want to ask questions, eat, use the bathroom, change money, get their baggage, or find a bus or taxi. How can airports help people who speak so many different languages? Can they have a person who speaks every language? Can they make very large signs to say *restaurant* in 20 languages? A better idea is to use a picture symbol that everyone can understand.

    a. Picture Symbols in International Hotels
    b. Fun Things to Do in a Hotel
    c. Finding a Good Hotel by Symbols

Symbols can help you find a good hotel. Many hotels want to have international visitors. They use picture symbols in advertising. Do you want a hotel with a swimming pool, tennis, a bar or a restaurant? You can look at the pictures to see if your hotel has these things.

    a. Symbols Can Help Keep You Safe
    b. Be Careful in Another Country
    c. Bad Things Can Happen

Sometimes bad things can happen to you in another country. You need to know the signs of danger so that you can be careful. Then if you hurt yourself, you need to know the signs for first aid or hospital so you can get help.

Timed Reading

Directions: *Read the timed reading again. Your teacher will time your reading. Put your reading rate on Chart 2 in the back of this book.*

Timed Reading Comprehension Check

Directions: *1. Answer all the questions about the timed reading.*
             2. Go back to the timed reading and check your answers. Put a line under the answer in the timed reading. In the blank, write the line number where you found the answer in the timed reading.

3. *When you have finished, your teacher may ask you to talk about the answers in a small group. In your group, try to agree on the answers, and then report back to the class.*

Line Number	*Answer*	*True/False:*
——	——	1. It took more than 10 years for Pioneer 10 to leave the solar system.
——	——	2. It is very easy to send something out of the solar system.
——	——	3. Scientists think there may be living things on Mars or Jupiter.
——	——	4. Living things from space can probably find us if they look at the pictures on Pioneer 10.
——	——	5. We will not be living when Pioneer 10 goes near the next star and sends back pictures.

Directions: *Choose one word from the list to put in each blank.*

World's Fair	hieroglyphics
leaves	possible
alphabet	represents

1. The word book _____ the idea of the thing you are holding in your hand.

2. Some letters of the _____ are x, m, and t.

3. In autumn in the northern part of the United States, the color of the _____ changes from green to red and yellow.

4. It is _____ there are living things in space.

5. Egyptians wrote in _____.

6. I visited the _____ in Vancouver, Canada, in 1986.

chapter 3 _____

Maps

Introduction

Directions: *Talk about these questions before you read the story.*

When have you used a map?
What does a map tell you?
Why is a map easy to understand?

Directions: *Read the story quickly. Try to guess the meaning of new words. Don't use your dictionary.*

A map is a drawing of part of the earth. A map does not show everything that a photograph shows. It shows only those things that are important to the people using the map.

Colors on maps tell us important things about the earth's surface. Things made by humans, such as cities, railroads, and highways, are usually black. Blue is the color for water. Rivers, lakes, and oceans are blue. Green is the color for trees and national parks.

A map symbol is a drawing that represents something real on the earth.

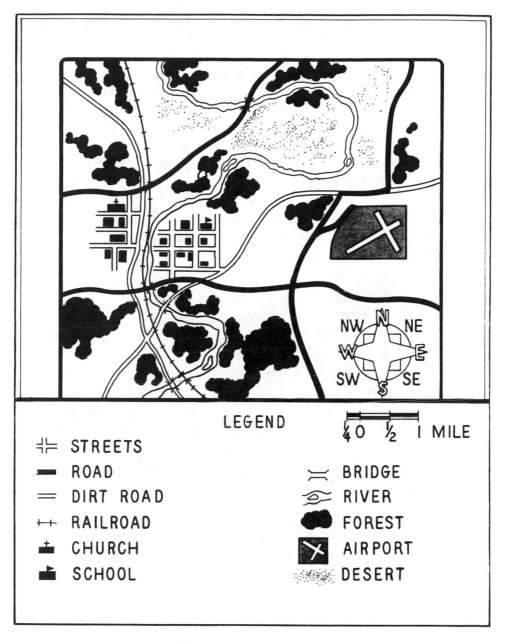

Figure 9   Small area map

On our map there are symbols for a house, church, and school. A box in the corner of the map tells what the symbols mean. We call the box a *legend*.

Maps of small areas can show each street, river, railroad, church, and school. Maps of larger areas show only the larger cities and roads. On larger area maps, you can see whole states or countries. You do not usually see streets or buildings on larger area maps.

One way to tell direction on a map is to look for the compass. The compass is a drawing showing directions. Usually, but not always, north is at the top of the map. When north is at the top, south is at the bottom. East is to the right, and west is to the left. The four other directions shown on the compass are northeast, southeast, southwest and northwest.

The map scale can tell you how far it is between any two places on the map. It is usually at the bottom or in a corner of the map. It tells you that a certain distance, such as an inch on the map, is equal to a certain number of miles or kilometers.

Because a map is like a picture, you can find out many things about an area more quickly than reading in books. You can find the answers to these questions quickly on a map:

1. Is the area near an ocean?
2. What other forms of water does it have?
3. Are there any mountains?
4. Is there a desert?
5. How far is it between cities?
6. What is the best way to travel between cities?
7. Are there any national parks or recreation areas?

Thousands of years ago, people made maps when they went to new places. They drew them on the earth or on walls of caves. Maps are better now because all maps begin from a photograph. Map photographs can be taken from airplanes or satellites. Today there are good maps of all areas of the world. There are even good maps of places difficult to travel to, such as the Arctic and Antarctica.

New maps are made every year because places change quickly. Every year there are new roads, bigger cities, and fewer trees.

When you travel, a map is very important. You can find where you want to go in a new place.

Check Your Guess

Directions: *You guessed the meaning of these words from this story. Circle the letter beside the answer that gives the same idea as the new word.*

1. A <u>square</u> in the corner explains the symbols. We call it a legend.
   a. a story
   b. a box
   c. a corner

2. The compass is a <u>symbol</u> showing directions.
   a. a machine
   b. north, south, east, west
   c. a drawing

3. The compass is a drawing showing <u>directions</u>. Usually north is at the top of the map, south is at the bottom, east is to the right, and west is to the left.
   a. north, south, east, west
   b. a drawing
   c. a symbol

4. The map <u>scale</u> tells you that an inch on the map is equal to a certain number of miles or kilometers on the earth.
   a. how much it weighs
   b. how far
   c. where

5. On large <u>area</u> maps, you can see whole states or countries.
   a. city
   b. paper
   c. place

6. Map photographs can be taken from airplanes or <u>satellites</u>.
   a. machines that circle the earth
   b. airplanes
   c. spaceships

Comprehension Exercises

Part 1: *You can find the answers to these questions in the story. You may look back to find an answer if you don't remember.*

1. What do the following colors on a map represent?
   black:
   blue:
   green:

2. What tells what the symbols mean?

3. How do all maps begin?

Figure 10   Map of Arizona

4. How often are new maps made?

Part 2: *You may not find the answers to these questions in the story, but you can answer the questions if you understand the ideas.*

1. Using the map scale on the map in Figure 9, how far is it from the airport to the church? From the school to the church? From the railroad to the airport?

2. Are there any canyons, lakes, or national parks in Arizona?

3. From Phoenix, what direction do you travel to the Grand Canyon in Arizona?

4. How do you think maps of Antarctica are made?

Comprehension Check

Directions: *Read each sentence. write T if it is true. Write F if it is false. Do not look back in the story.*

_____ 1. A map shows everything.

_____ 2. A legend tells you that an inch is equal to a certain number of miles or kilometers.

_____ 3. North is always at the top of a map.

_____ 4. Black is the color of water on a map.

_____ 5. Every year there are more trees.

_____ 6. People started making maps in the last 100 years.

_____ 7. You can find national parks on a map.

_____ 8. A compass shows directions.

_____ 9. We do not have good maps of some places that are difficult to travel to.

_____10. A large area map shows houses, churches, and schools.

Discussion Activities

Directions: *Discuss these topics as a class or in a small group.*

1. Without first looking at a map, draw a map of your country. Put in the three largest cities, lakes or oceans, mountains, and deserts. Show it to the class.

2. Bring photographs or postcards from your last vacation or from your country. Show them to the class and tell about them.

3. Tell whether you need a large area map or a small area map to go to these places:
   a. downtown
   b. Mexico
   c. your friend's house
   d. San Francisco

4. Find these mountain ranges on a world map:
   a. Alps
   b. Carpathians
   c. Pyrenees

5. Look at the map of Arizona. Tell how to get to the Grand Canyon from Tucson.

6. Work in pairs. The first person begins at a point on a map. He or she gives directions to another point on the map. The second person follows on his or her map and guesses the final destination on the map. Then switch. The second person gives directions, and the first person follows. Use the small area map and the map of Arizona in your book.

TIMED READING

Mapping the Moon

Directions: *Read quickly. Your teacher will time you. Put your reading rate on Chart 1 in the back of this book.*

In 1610, the famous Italian scientist Galileo made the first	10
telescope. He looked at the moon with the telescope. He was surprised	22
to see deep craters, mountains, and dark smooth areas he thought were	34
seas. Today we know they are not water. They are large craters.	46
In the 1600s, Galileo named some of the places on the moon and	59
made the first map of the moon. Craters were named after philosophers,	71
such as Tycho, Plato, Copernicus, Kepler, and Aristotle. The dark areas	82
were given names such as Sea of Showers, Sea of Tranquility, and Sea of	96

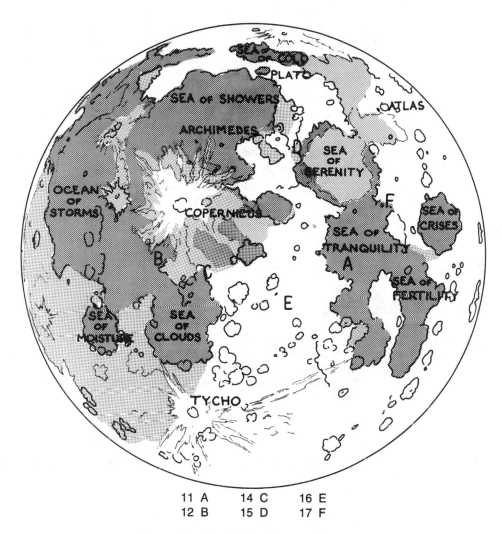

| 11 A | 14 C | 16 E |
| 12 B | 15 D | 17 F |

Figure 11   Apollo landings on the moon

Serenity. The early names were in Latin because Latin was the scientific   108
language of the time.   112

There are also mountains on the moon. The mountains on the   123
moon were named after mountains on earth. There are Alps,   133
Carpathians and Pyrenees on the moon as well as on the earth.   145

Astronauts first went to the moon on the Apollo missions in the   157
late 1960s and the early 1970s. They were going to a place for the first   172
time. They needed a map. Scientists wanted better maps of the moon   184
than they could get from earth. Scientists from both the United States   196
and Russia sent many unmanned spaceships to the moon. These   206
spaceships had television cameras to send pictures back to earth. The   217

cameras took pictures until the moment the spacecraft crashed on the   228
moon. They sent back closeup pictures of the moon. With these   239
pictures, scientists were able to find good places for the astronauts to 251
land on the moon on the Apollo trips.   259

There were six Apollo trips to the moon. The astronauts took even   271
better pictures of the moon on these trips. Now we have good maps of   285
the moon.   287

It is difficult to make maps of space because the planets and stars   300
are so far away. When we find ways to send spacecraft to take better   314
pictures, we can make better maps. These maps will be very important   326
to people who travel into space in the future.   335

READING SKILLS EXERCISES

Using the Context

Directions: *You don't always need to know all of the words in a story. You can still understand the ideas. Read the following paragraph or paragraphs. Don't worry about the blanks at first. Answer the true/false questions for all paragraphs. Then go back and fill in the blanks, choosing a word from the following list.*

It is very difficult to make maps of space. The stars and planets are very far apart, and everything is always moving. Looking into space is like looking into the past. Nothing is where you see it. Light _____ at a speed of 186,300 miles per second. Light comes from the sun to the earth in about eight minutes. Light comes from the _____ star in about three years. The sun and stars are not where we see them. By the time their light gets to earth, they may have moved _____ of miles.

_____ A star is not in the place where we see the light.

The earth turns around one time each day, and it travels around the sun. Most _____ and stars move, too. The map-maker takes a picture to make a map. He or she stops everything for one _____ in time. The map will only be _____ for a very short time.

_____ It is not necessary to change space maps often.

We can't make a _____ map of space; yet, people have always
₁
wanted to see a picture of where they are going. They like to have a map so they

can show where they are and where they have been. A new _____ of
₂
mapping has been made for space. The Milky Way is the center of space maps,

not the earth's equator. Space maps will look like an _____ plans for a
₃
tall building. A different map will be made for each _____ of the
₄
building.

_____ Space maps are the same as earth maps.

nearest	moment
correct	travels
way	flat
planets	billions
floor	architect's

Timed Reading

Directions: _Read the timed reading again. Your teacher will time your reading. Put your reading rate on Chart 2 in the back of this book._

Timed Reading Comprehension Check

Directions: 1. _Answer all the questions about the timed reading._
2. _Go back to the timed reading and check your answers. Put a line under the answer in the timed reading. In the blank, write the line number where you found the answer in the timed reading._
3. _When you have finished, your teacher may ask you to talk about the answers in a small group. In your group, try to agree on the answers and then report back to the class._

Line Number	Answer	True/False:
_____	_____	1. There is no water on the moon.
_____	_____	2. Carpathian was a philosopher.

___ ___ 3. The names of the mountains on the moon are the same as on earth.

___ ___ 4. It was expensive to get good pictures to make maps of the moon for the astronauts.

___ ___ 5. Unmanned spaceships brought back pictures of the moon.

Directions: *Choose one word from the list to put in each blank.*

> area   compass
> legend   directions
>   satellites

1. In a _____ for a map of the moon, we would only see symbols for craters, mountains, and seas.

2. _____ take pictures of the earth. They were not very good for taking pictures of the moon.

3. Apollo 11 landed in an _____ near the Sea of Tranquility.

4. If you get lost when you travel, stop and ask for _____.

5. Look at the _____ to find north.

SUPPLEMENTAL READING

Maps for Study

Directions: *Your teacher may use this as a timed reading in class or let you read it by yourself outside of class.*

Maps can help students. In books, maps can often give information	11
in a picture much more quickly and clearly than words. Maps can show	24
information about history, politics, oil and minerals, population,	32
weather, winds, ocean currents, kinds of food grown on farms, kinds of	44
trees, languages, religions, economy, manufacturing, transportation,	50
exports and imports, and many other topics. Farmers and business	60
people as well as students need this information for their work.	71
In order to show this information to students, the map-maker must	82
first gather geographic information. Then he or she uses an easy-to-read	95
map and chooses only the information needed to show his or her idea. A	109
map is different from a photograph because a photograph shows	119
everything. The map shows only what the map-maker wants to tell us.	131

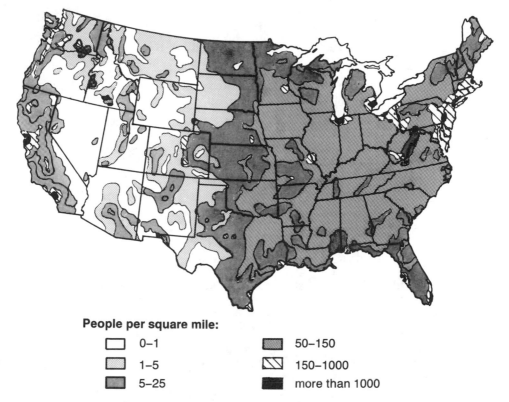

People per square mile:

☐	0–1	▨	50–150
▨	1–5	◺	150–1000
■	5–25	■	more than 1000

Figure 12 Population of the United States

For example, maybe the map-maker wants to show how much rain   142
falls in different parts of the United States. The map-maker starts with   154
an outline of the United States. He or she does not put in cities, rivers,   169
lakes, or other things. The map-maker only wants to show us rainfall.   181

Then the map-maker chooses symbols for different amounts of   190
rain. Different colors are very good symbols to use. In black-and-white   203
books other symbols must be used, such as lines, dots, dashes, shapes   215
such as circles and triangles, and only the colors black and white.   227

With practice, you can become good at reading maps. It is most   239
important to learn how to read the explanation of the symbols in the   252
legend.   253

Comprehension Questions

Directions: *Look at the maps to find the answers to these questions.*

True/False:

_____ 1. Texas became part of the United States in 1803.

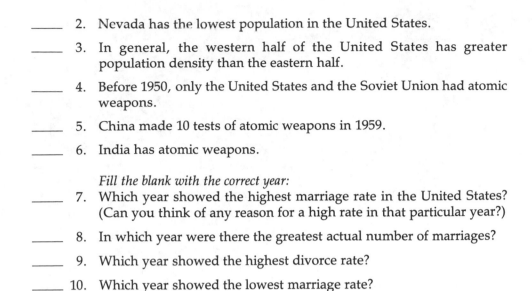

_____ 2. Nevada has the lowest population in the United States.

_____ 3. In general, the western half of the United States has greater population density than the eastern half.

_____ 4. Before 1950, only the United States and the Soviet Union had atomic weapons.

_____ 5. China made 10 tests of atomic weapons in 1959.

_____ 6. India has atomic weapons.

Fill the blank with the correct year:

_____ 7. Which year showed the highest marriage rate in the United States? (Can you think of any reason for a high rate in that particular year?)

_____ 8. In which year were there the greatest actual number of marriages?

_____ 9. Which year showed the highest divorce rate?

_____ 10. Which year showed the lowest marriage rate?

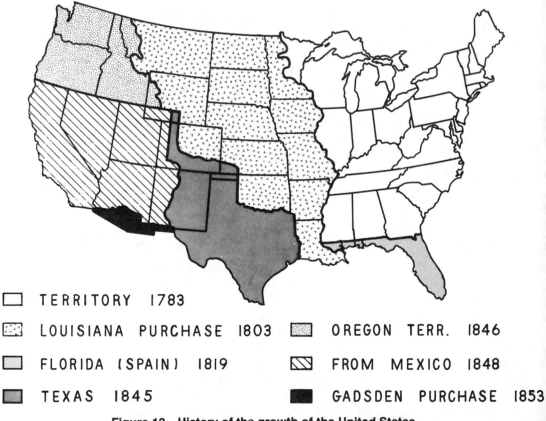

☐ TERRITORY 1783

▨ LOUISIANA PURCHASE 1803   ▨ OREGON TERR. 1846

☐ FLORIDA (SPAIN) 1819   ▨ FROM MEXICO 1848

◼ TEXAS 1845   ◼ GADSDEN PURCHASE 1853

Figure 13   History of the growth of the United States

Figure 14 Nuclear Weapons Tests (known nuclear tests, 1945–1987)

	United States	Soviet Union	Britain	France	China
1945–49	8	1	0	0	0
1950–59	188	89	21	0	0
1960–69	344	168	4	30	10
1970–79	162	198	5	57	5
1980–87	125	157	11	70	6
Total	827	626	41	157	31

Note: India reported one test in 1974.

Figure 15 Marriage and Divorce Rates in the United States

	Marriages		Divorces			Marriages		Divorces	
Year	Num.	Rate	Num.	Rate	Year	Num.	Rate	Num.	Rate
1895	620,000	8.9	40,387	0.6	1945	1,612,992	12.2	485,000	3.5
1900	709,000	9.3	55,751	0.7	1950	1,667,231	11.1	385,144	2.6
1905	842,000	10.0	67,976	0.8	1955	1,531,000	9.3	377,000	2.3
1910	948,166	10.3	83,045	0.9	1960	1,523,000	8.5	393,000	2.2
1915	1,007,595	10.0	104,298	1.0	1965	1,800,000	9.3	479,000	2.5
1920	1,274,476	12.0	170,505	1.6	1970	2,158,802	10.6	708,000	3.5
1925	1,188,334	10.3	175,449	1.5	1975	2,152,662	10.0	1,036,000	4.8
1930	1,126,856	9.2	195,961	1.6	1980	2,413,000	10.6	1,182,000	5.2
1935	1,327,000	10.4	218,000	1.7	1985	2,425,000	10.2	1,187,000	5.0
1940	1,595,879	12.1	264,000	2.0	1987	2,421,000	9.9	1,157,000	4.8

chapter 4 _____

The Namib Desert

Introduction

Directions: *Talk about these questions before you read the story.*

Look at the picture of the desert.
What is a desert like?
Have you ever visited a desert? Tell the class about it.
How many deserts can you name?
Find them on a map and show them to the class.
What can you find in a desert?

Directions: *Read the story quickly. Try to guess the meaning of new words. Don't use your dictionary.*

Sand is everywhere, as far as you can see. Does anything live in a place like this?

People who live near this desert say that nothing can live here. They say that it is empty. Scientists say that they are wrong. There is life here. There is not much rain in the desert, but sometimes it is full of living things.

Figure 16   A desert

The empty place is the Namib Desert in southwestern Africa. It stretches for 1,300 miles along the Atlantic Ocean. The desert is from 50 to 100 miles wide.

Scientists know this desert very well. They say that the Namib has more unusual plants and animals than any other desert in the world.

All the plants and animals in the Namib are alike in two important ways. They can live on very little water, and they can live in very hot weather.

Figure 17   A beetle

Figure 18　A desert bird and a baobab tree

Most of the time in the Namib, there are no clouds to hide the sun. The sun shines down all day and makes the sand very hot. Sometimes years go by before rain cools the sand. When it rains, plants grow in the sand very quickly.

Desert plants and animals need some water. It does not rain much in the desert. The water they need comes from <u>fog</u>.* The fog comes in from the ocean about 60 days each year.

When this happens, some animals catch the small drops of water that make the fog. One kind of beetle gets water to drink from the fog. The fog makes drops of water on the beetle's body. The drops run down toward the beetle's mouth. Then the beetle drinks them.

Some desert animals do not wait for the water to come to them. The water is miles away, but they go after it. Each morning, birds fly to water holes as far away as 50 miles. They drink. Then they wet their <u>feathers</u>† to carry water back to their baby birds.

Some plants, like the baobab tree, can live for a long time without water. The baobab tree holds water in its trunk. The sun does not hurt the top of the baobab tree because it does not have many leaves. It can live 4,000 years. It is one of the oldest living things on earth.

Some scientists want to live in the Namib Desert because it is interesting. More than 300 scientists live there and study the strange life on the hot sands. They think that life in the desert can be both interesting and difficult.

*fog–small drops of water in the air, like a cloud near the ground
†feathers–what covers the outside of a bird

Check Your Guess

Directions: *You guessed the meaning of these words from this story. Circle the letter beside the answer that gives the same idea as the new word. Do not use a dictionary.*

1. The water comes from <u>fog</u>. The fog comes in from the ocean about 60 days each year.
   a. rain
   b. river
   c. clouds in the air near the earth

2. The birds fly to water holes as far away as 50 miles. They drink. They wet their <u>feathers</u> to carry water back to their baby birds.
   a. the birds' mouths
   b. the birds' feet
   c. the birds' covering

3. Look at the desert. <u>Sand</u> is everywhere, as far as you can see.
   a. very small pieces of rock
   b. very small pieces of wood
   c. very small bits of water

4. When this happens, some animals catch the small drops of water that make the fog. One kind of beetle gets water to drink from the fog. The fog makes <u>drops</u> of water on the beetle's body.
   a. small pieces of rock
   b. small bits of water
   c. small pieces of wood

5. All the plants and animals in the Namib are <u>alike</u> in two important ways. They can live on very little water, and they can live in very hot weather.
   a. alive
   b. different
   c. the same

Comprehension Exercises

Part 1: *You can find the answers to these questions in the story. You may look back to find an answer if you don't remember.*

1. Where is the Namib Desert? How big is it?

2. What must plants and animals be like in the desert?

3. How do plants and animals get water in the Namib?

4. How many scientists live in the Namib? Why?

Part 2: *You may not find the answers to these questions in the story, but you can answer the questions if you understand the ideas.*

1. Tell how beetles get water in the Namib Desert.

2. Do you think beetles have soft or hard bodies? Why?

3. Tell how baby birds get water in the Namib Desert.

4. Do all deserts have fog? Why does the Namib Desert have fog?

Comprehension Check

Directions: *Read each sentence. Write T if it is true. Write F if it is false. Do not look back in the story.*

_____ 1. The Namib Desert is empty.

_____ 2. The Namib Desert is in North Africa.

_____ 3. There are more unusual plants and animals in the Namib Desert than in any other desert.

_____ 4. Any kind of plant can live in the desert.

_____ 5. The sand in the desert is almost always very hot during the day.

_____ 6. Fog comes in from the ocean almost every day.

_____ 7. Birds carry water in their mouths back to their babies.

_____ 8. A baobab tree can live a long time without water because it holds water in its trunk.

_____ 9. A baobab tree can live 6,000 years.

_____ 10. Nobody lives in the desert.

Discussion Activities

Directions: *Discuss these topics as a class or in a small group.*

1. What can be dangerous about a desert? What would you like and dislike about living in a desert?

2. Why is it difficult to travel in a desert?

3. How do you think the 300 scientists can live in the desert? What do they need? What kinds of houses do you think they have? Where do they get water?

TIMED READING

What Makes a Desert?

Directions: *Read quickly. Your teacher will time you. Put your reading rate on Chart 1 in the back of this book.*

Scientists are trying to make the deserts into good land again. They	12
want to bring water to the deserts so people can live and grow food.	26
They are learning a lot about the deserts. Even so, more and more of the	41
earth is becoming desert all the time. Scientists may not be able to	54
change the deserts in time.	59
Why is more and more land becoming desert? Scientists think that	70
people make deserts. People are doing bad things to the earth.	81
Some places on the earth do not get very much rain. Yet, they still	95
do not become deserts. This is because there are some green plants	107
growing there. Small green plants and grass are very important to dry	119
places. Plants help keep water in the earth. Plants do not let the wind	133
blow the dirt away. When a little bit of rain falls, the plants hold the	148
water. Without plants, the land can become a desert much more easily.	159
A man decides to make a farm in a very dry place. He cuts down	174
the trees. He digs in the earth and takes away the grass and plants that	189
are already growing on the dry land.	196
He makes a farm. He puts plants in rows. The sun is very hot. It	211
makes the land even drier. When the rain comes, it runs between the	224
rows of plants. It washes the good dirt away. When the wind comes, it	240
blows between the rows of plants. It blows the good dirt away.	252

Figure 19   A farm with plants in rows

Soon the land is not good enough for a farm anymore. The man   265
lets his animals eat all the plants on it. Now the land does not have any   281
plants on it. The sun and wind dry the land and blow all of the good dirt   298
away. Now the land is a desert.   305

READING SKILLS EXERCISES

Reading to Find Information

Directions: *Read the question. Then move your eyes over the paragraph that follows it. It is not necessary to read every word carefully. Just look for the answer to the question. Put a line under the answer. Work quickly.*

What does a man take from the land?

A man decides to make a farm in a very dry place. He cuts down the trees. He digs in the earth and takes away the grass and plants that are already growing on the dry land. He makes a farm. He plants in rows.

What does a man see that means there is water?

A man is lost in the desert. He walks in the morning and evening. He sleeps in the middle of the day. It is very hot. He has a little water to drink. At the top of each hill, he looks for anything—a tree, a house, a fire. He watches the sun so he knows he is walking north. Finally, on the ninth day he sees some green trees far away. He knows there is water there. He is safe!

Reading to Find the Main Idea

Directions: *Read the three titles. Then read the paragraph. Choose the title that is best for the whole paragraph.*

  a. Bringing Water to the Desert
  b. Scientists Work Against Time in the Desert
  c. How to Make a Desert

  Scientists are trying to make the desert into good land again. They want to bring water to the deserts so people can live and grow food. They are learning a lot about the deserts. Even so, more and more land is becoming desert all the time. Scientists may not be able to change the deserts in time.

Using the Context

Directions: *You don't always need to know all of the words in a story. You can still understand the ideas. Read the following paragraph or paragraphs. Don't worry about the blanks at first. Answer the true/false questions for all paragraphs. Then go back and fill in the blanks, choosing a word from the following list.*

  Some places on the earth do not get very much rain. Yet, they still do not become deserts. This is because there are some green plants growing there. Green plant cover is very important to _____ places. Plants help keep
  1
water in the earth. Plants do not let the wind blow the dirt away. When a little bit of rain falls, the plants _____ the water. Without plants, the land can
  2
become a desert much more _____.
  3

_____Plants can keep dry land from becoming desert.

  Soon the _____ is not good enough for a farm anymore. The man
  1
lets his animals eat all the plants on it. Now the land does not have any plants on it. The _____ and wind dry the land and blow all of the good
  2
_____ away. Now the land is a desert.
  3

_____ It is bad to make a farm in a dry place, but it is good to raise animals there.

sun	dirt
hold	easily
dry	land

Timed Reading

Directions: 1. *Answer all the questions about the timed reading.*
2. *Go back to the timed reading and check your answers. Put a line under the answer in the timed reading. In the blank, write the line number where you found the answer in the timed reading.*
3. *When you have finished, your teacher may ask you to talk about the answers in a small group. In your group, try to agree on the answers and then report back to the class.*

Line
Number   *Answer*

_____   _____   1. Land is becoming desert because of
- a. not enough rain.
- b. not enough wind.
- c. people.

_____   _____   2. Small green plants are very important to dry places because
- a. they keep the earth from becoming even drier.
- b. they do not let the wind blow the earth away.
- c. they hold water.
- d. all of the above.

True/False

_____   _____   3. It is bad to plant in rows in a dry place.

_____   _____   4. It is better to raise animals on dry land than to plant a farm.

_____   _____   5. All places that don't get very much rain are deserts.

Directions: *Choose one word from the list to put in each blank.*

fog	feathers
sand	drops
alike	

1. Most deserts look _____ because there are not many plants, and there is a lot of _____.

2. The _____ of some birds are very beautiful.

3. London has a lot of _____, but the Sahara Desert does not.

4. Rain _____ are not very usual in the Namib Desert.

Word Families Vocabulary Exercise

Directions: *Words have different forms depending on how they are used in a sentence, but the meaning of the word usually doesn't change. You can increase your vocabulary by recognizing the different forms of a word.*

Noun	Verb	Adjective	Adverb
science scientist		scientific	scientifically
representation representative	represent	representative unrepresentative	
possibility		possible	possibly
symbol symbolism	symbolize	symbolic	symbolically
interest	interest	interesting	interestingly
reflection	reflect	reflective	reflectively
life	live	living	
student	study	studious	studiously
knowledge	know	knowing	knowingly
information	inform	informed	

Directions: *Choose the correct form of one of the words above to fill in the blanks.*

1. Juan is a _____ at the University of Arizona, where he wants to _____ biology.

2. _____ do not _____ for sure if there is _____ in space.

3. Pioneer 10 is still sending us much _____ about space.

4. When we look in a mirror, we can see our _____.

5. The dove, a kind of bird, is a _____ of peace.

chapter 5 _____

A History of Telling Time

Introduction

Directions: *Talk about these questions before you read the story.*

Are you sometimes late?

Do you try to be on time?

When is it important to be on time?

How can you tell what time it is? Tell some different ways.

Directions: *Read the story quickly. Try to guess the meaning of new words. Don't use your dictionary.*

What time is it? There are many ways you can find out the time. You may have a wristwatch on your arm. You can look at an alarm clock beside your bed. People tell the time on the radio or TV. You can call a number on the telephone and get the time.

It has not always been easy to know the time. A long time ago people looked at the sun to tell the time. The sun was their clock. They could tell the time of day by the place of the sun in the sky: morning, noon, or afternoon.

After many years people began to see something else about the sun. When the sun shone on something, it made a dark shadow behind it. This was the place that did not get sunlight. As the sun moved across the sky, the shadow moved too. People could tell time better by the shadows than by the sun. They made something long and pointed so that the shadow was easier to see.

An example of shadow clocks are the obelisks from Egypt. They are tall, thin buildings that come to a point at the top. Cleopatra's Needles are the two most famous obelisks in the world. They are almost 3,500 years old. One of them is now in Central Park in New York City.

About the same time, people began to make sundials. Sundials have a round part. A long, thin point is in the center. There are twelve lines in the round part to <u>divide</u>* the day into twelve parts.

Around the year 1250, someone made the first mechanical clock. It was a mechanical clock because it was a machine that ran by itself. It did not need the help of anything in nature.

People began to use the hourglass clock around the year 1400. They made it from glass. It was wide at the top and bottom but narrow in the middle. They put some sand in one part. The sand ran from the top part to the bottom part of the glass in one hour. At the end of every hour people turned the glass over and began again.

Figure 20   An obelisk

*divide—cut into parts of the same size

Figure 21　A sundial

People carried the first watches in their pockets. Then during World War I men started wearing their watches on their wrists, not in their pockets. It was easier and faster to tell the time. Now almost everyone wears a wristwatch.

Many other clocks run on electricity. Electric clocks run better than most other clocks.

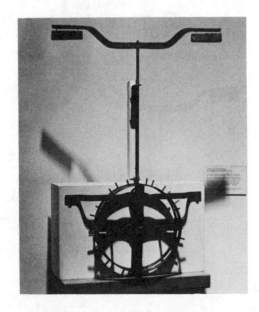

Figure 22　The first mechanical clock

Figure 23   An hourglass

Today people want to know the exact time. Exact means that the time is not a few minutes before or after, but the correct time. Radio, TV, trains, airplanes, science, and business need to know that they have the same time.

Scientists have atomic clocks. They keep the exact time for the rest of the world. Atomic clocks are very exact. If they run for 3,000 years, they will not be more than one second slow. They are very expensive. The atomic clock at the

Figure 24   An atomic clock

National Bureau of Standards in Boulder, Colorado, keeps time for the western United States and cost several million dollars to make. Now you, too, can buy an atomic clock. Smaller ones are available commercially for about $10,000 to $50,000.

Check Your Guess

Directions: *You guessed the meaning of these words from this story. Circle the letter beside the answer that gives the same idea as the new word. Do not use a dictionary.*

1. When the sun shone on something, it made a dark <u>shadow</u> behind it. This was the place that did not get sunlight.
   a. a place that did not get water
   b. a dark place that did not get sunlight
   c. a tall, thin, pointed building

2. People could tell time better by the shadows than by the sun. They made something long and pointed so that the shadow was <u>easier</u> to see.
   a. not difficult
   b. unusual
   c. tall

3. Sundials have a round part. A long, thin point is in the center. There are 12 lines in the round part to <u>divide</u> the day into 12 parts.
   a. find
   b. start
   c. cut

4. An hourglass was made from glass. It was wide at the top and bottom but <u>narrow</u> in the middle.
   a. tall
   b. not wide
   c. big

5. Around the year 1250, someone made the first <u>mechanical</u> clock. It was a mechanical clock because it was a machine that ran by itself. It did not need the help of anything in nature.
   a. It ran by machine.
   b. It ran by nature.
   c. It did not run.

Comprehension Exercises

Part 1: *You can find the answers to these questions in the story. You may look back to find an answer if you don't remember.*

1. How did people first tell time?

2. How old are the oldest clocks?

3. How is a mechanical clock different from other clocks?

4. Why did people start to wear their watches on their wrists?

5. How exact are atomic clocks?

6. How much does an atomic clock cost?

Part 2: *You may not find the answers to these questions in the story, but you can answer the questions if you understand the ideas.*

1. Can you think of a problem with telling time with sundials and obelisks?

2. Can you think of a problem with telling time with an hourglass?

3. Why is it necessary to have exact time?

4. Can you think of a problem with using electric clocks? Why are they better than most other clocks?

5. Which is a mechanical clock?
   a. sundial
   b. hourglass
   c. electric clock
   d. obelisk

6. Which is the most exact?
   a. an electric clock
   b. an atomic clock
   c. a wristwatch
   d. a pocketwatch

Comprehension Check

Directions: *Read each sentence. Write T if it is true. Write F if it is false. Do not look back in the story.*

_____ 1. People could tell time better by the sun than by shadows.

_____ 2. Early sundials divided the day into 12 parts.

_____ 3. A mechanical clock does not need the help of anything in nature.

_____ 4. An hourglass has water in it.

_____ 5. Wristwatches began to be used during World War II.

_____ 6. All atomic clocks are in the United States.

_____ 7. Atomic clocks are cheap.

_____ 8. Electric clocks probably run better than pocketwatches.

_____ 9. Electric clocks are the most exact.

_____ 10. Anyone can find out the exact time from an atomic clock.

Discussion Activities

Directions: *Discuss these topics as a class or in a small group.*

1. How do you think one of Cleopatra's Needles got to New York City?

2. Why do you think people are so interested in telling time? Is it important to be on time?

3. How many ways of telling time do you have? How many ways do you use in a day, a week, etc.?

4. Try to find a telephone number for a recorded message telling the correct time and temperature. Call the number and tell the class about it.

Time Zones

Directions: *Read quickly. Your teacher will time you. Put your reading rate on Chart 1 in the back of this book.*

Before 1883, most cities in the United States had their own time.	12
They set their time by the sun. This made many problems for the	25
railroad companies. Their trains went to more than 300 different cities.	36
Every city had a different time.	42

In 1883, William Allen made a plan to divide the United States into 55
four different parts, called *time zones*. This made things easier for the 67
railroad companies. Now every city in the same time zone has the same 80
time. The map shows the time zones. They are Pacific Standard Time 92
(PST), Mountain Standard Time (MST), Central Standard Time (CST), 101
and Eastern Standard Time (EST). The clocks above the map tell the time 114
in each zone. 117

Today, most parts of the United States have daylight saving time 128
for almost seven months of the year. People want to have more daylight 140
hours after work. They want to have fun outdoors during this time. 152
People turn their clocks forward one hour before they go to bed on the 166
first Saturday in April. They turn them back one hour before they go to 180
bed on the last Saturday in October. 187

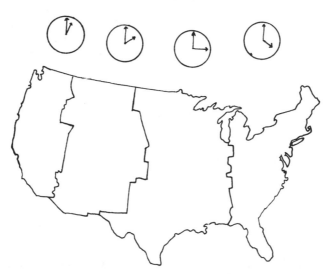

Figure 25   Time zones in the United States

We can't really save an hour of daylight to use when we need it. We   202
can change only what the clock says. Before we changed the clock for   215
daylight saving time, it was dark in the evening at seven o'clock. With   228
daylight saving time, it is daylight at seven in the evening but dark at   242
eight o'clock. Before we changed the clock, it was light in the morning at   256
five o'clock. With daylight saving time, it gets light at six o'clock in the 270
morning. Of course, the number of daylight hours is the same.   281

READING SKILLS EXERCISES

Reading to Find Information

Directions: *Read the question. Then move your eyes over the paragraph that follows it. It is not necessary to read every word carefully. Just look for the answer to the question. Put a line under the answer. Work quickly.*

How long is daylight saving time?

Today most parts of the United States have daylight saving time for almost seven months of the year. People want to have more daylight hours after work. They want to have fun outdoors because the weather is good. People turn their clocks forward one hour before going to bed on the first Saturday in April. They turn them back one hour before they go to bed on the last Saturday in October.

Why do we need daylight saving time in December?

Today many people want daylight saving time all year long. Without daylight saving time in November and December, in some places it is dark when children go home from school at 4:30 P.M. It is dark when people go home from work at 5:00 P.M.

Reading to Find the Main Idea

Directions: *Read the three titles. Then read the paragraph. Choose the title that is best for the whole paragraph.*

   a. Changing Only the Clocks
   b. Really Saving an Hour
   c. Making More Hours in the Day

We can't really save an hour of daylight to use when we need it. We can change only what the clock says. Before we changed the clock for daylight saving time, it was dark in the evening at seven o'clock. With daylight saving time, it is daylight at seven o'clock in the evening but dark at eight o'clock. Before we changed the clock, it was light in the morning at five o'clock. With daylight saving time, it gets light at six o'clock. Of course, the number of daylight hours is the same.

Using the Context

Directions: *You don't always need to know all of the words in a story. You can still understand the ideas. Read the following paragraph or paragraphs. Don't worry about the blanks at first. Answer the true/false question for all paragraphs. Then go back and fill in the blanks, choosing a word from the following list.*

We can't really save an hour of daylight to _____ when we need it. We can change only what the clock says. Before we changed the clock for daylight saving time, it was dark in the evening at seven o'clock. With daylight saving time, it is daylight at seven o'clock but dark at eight o'clock. Before we changed the clock, _____ was dark in the morning at five o'clock. With daylight saving time, it becomes light at six o'clock. Of course, the daylight hours _____ the same.

_____ With daylight saving time, it stays daylight in the evening one
   hour less.

In 1883, William Allen made a plan to _____ the United States into four different _____, called *time zones*. This made things easier for the railroad _____. Now every city in the same time zone has the same time.

_____ Every city in the same time zone has a different time.

made	companies
by	divide
outdoors	remain
parts	daybreak
	have

Timed Reading

Directions: *Read the timed reading again. Your teacher will time your reading. Put your reading rate on Chart 2 in the back of this book.*

Timed Reading Comprehension Check

Directions: 1. *Answer all the questions about the timed reading.*

2. *Go back to the timed reading and check your answers. Put a line under the answer in the timed reading. In the blank, write the line number where you found the answer in the timed reading.*

3. *When you have finished, your teacher may ask you to talk about the answers in a small group. In your group try to agree on the answers, and then report back to the class.*

Line
Number   *Answer*

_____   _____   1. Daylight saving time is in
　　　　　　　　　　　　　 a. winter.　　　　　d. March.
　　　　　　　　　　　　　 b. November.　　　e. all of the above.
　　　　　　　　　　　　　 c. summer.

_____   _____   2. People change their clocks in
　　　　　　　　　　　　　 a. April.　　　　　 d. November.
　　　　　　　　　　　　　 b. March　　　　　 e. both a and d.
　　　　　　　　　　　　　 c. September.

　　　　　　　　　　　　　 True/False

_____   _____   3. Time is different by one hour in each time zone.

_____   _____   4. We have daylight saving time so we can save an hour of daylight.

_____   _____   5. The United States is too large to have one time zone.

Directions: *Choose one word from the list to put in each blank.*

　　　　　　　mechanical　　　narrow
　　　　　　　easier　　　　　　divide
　　　　　　　shadow

1. With daylight saving time, we can still see our _____ at seven in the evening.

2. In 1883, William Allen made a plan to _____ the United States into four time zones. This made things _____ for the railroad companies.

3. The time zones are not _____ pieces of land; they can be several hundred miles wide.

4. _____ clocks are better than sundials.

chapter 6 _____

Weather Maps

Introduction

Directions: *Talk about these questions before you read the story.*

Do you like the weather today?

Do you know what the weather will be tomorrow?

How can you know what the weather will be tomorrow?

Will you be ready for a change in the weather?

Directions: *Read the story quickly. Try to guess the meaning of new words. Don't use your dictionary.*

The weather often changes what people do and how they do it. The weather is important every day in our lives. It may even change the way we feel and think.

Meteorologists are scientists who study the weather. They try to predict or forecast the weather. They need to know what the weather will be like tomorrow, next week, maybe next month. How do they find this information?

Figure 26 A satellite weather map

For a long time, scientists tried to predict the weather by looking at it. This does not work very well. If a man stands on a very high mountain, he can see only a small part of the weather. In 1820, a German scientist showed that scientists could draw a map of the way weather moves.

The weather of tomorrow is far away today. It may move as fast as 30 miles an hour. It may move 720 miles in 24 hours.

Because weather moves, the best way to predict it is to use maps. You can see a picture of the weather for large parts of the country on a map. Winter storms of rain and snow can be 1,000 miles wide. Meteorologists can see a storm this big only on a map.

In 1820, it was difficult to make these maps. It was not easy then to get weather reports quickly. The scientists needed the reports to make the maps. Today it is not difficult to get weather reports quickly from everywhere.

Today the whole world works together to make weather maps. Weather forecasters send reports from country to country in seconds. There are weather

Figure 27 Weather ships, airplanes, weather balloons, and satellites help the weathermen.

offices in many, many places. There are weather ships, planes, weather balloons, and satellites to help the weather forecasters. They use computers to make their maps. There is no need to draw the maps by hand. Storms, wind direction, temperature, barometric pressure, and humidity are put on a map by computer.

Weather forecasters study the weather 24 hours a day, seven days a week. All their reports will be on maps in New York, London, Tokyo, Mexico City, and many other places.

People in all these places speak different languages, but this is not a problem. Weather is international. That is, it has its own special language, and people in all countries can understand it. The weather forecasters draw maps in the same figures and numbers in all countries. A weather map from the United States and Canada looks the same as a map from Turkey, Russia, or Sweden.

Sometimes we plan what we will do the next day around the weather. We want to know what we can do or can't do. We watch television to find out the weather for tomorrow. We can listen to the radio or read the newspaper. Everyone all over the world can read the same maps. They can know about the weather. They can plan their days too.

Figure 28 Weathermen use computers to draw maps in the same figures and numbers in all countries.

Check Your Guess

Directions: *You guessed the meaning of these words from this story. Circle the letter beside the answer that gives the same idea as the new word. Do not use a dictionary.*

1. Today the whole world works <u>together</u> to make weather maps. Weather forecasters send reports from country to country in seconds.

   a. alone

   b. with each other

   c. not at all

2. Weather is <u>international</u>. That is, it has its own special language, and people in all countries can understand it.

   a. for some nations

   b. for all nations

   c. for no nations

3. Weather is international. That is, it has its own <u>special</u> language, and people in all countries can understand it.

   a. usual

   b. different

   c. difficult

4. Sometimes we <u>plan</u> what we will do the next day around the weather. We want to know what we can or can't do.

   a. think about the future

   b. change

   c. tell

5. Winter <u>storms</u> of rain and snow can be 1,000 miles wide. They can hurt people and things.

   a. good weather

   b. bad weather

   c. clear weather

6. Meteorologists try to <u>predict</u> the weather. They need to know what the weather will be like tomorrow, next week, maybe next month.

   a. understand the weather

   b. tell what will happen in the future

   c. remember the past weather

Comprehension Exercises

Part 1: *You can find the answers to these questions in the story. You may look back to find an answer if you don't remember.*

1. What do we call scientists who study the weather?

2. How did scientists predict the weather before 1820?

3. What happened in 1820 to change the way scientists predict the weather?

4. How fast can the weather move?

5. How large can some weather storms be?

Part 2: *You may not find the answers to these questions in the story, but you can answer the questions if you understand the ideas.*

1. How can meteorologists in all the different countries understand the weather?

2. How much of the weather can you really see?

3. How much of the weather can meteorologists see?

4. For some people it is very important to know what the weather will be tomorrow. Can you think of some people who need to know the weather more than others do?

Comprehension Check

Directions: *Read each sentence. Write T if it is true. Write F if it is false. Do not look back in the story.*

_____ 1. Meteorologists only study storms.

_____ 2. A storm may move 720 miles an hour.

_____ 3. In 1720, a German scientist showed that scientists could draw a map of the weather.

_____ 4. Winter storms can be 1,000 miles wide.

_____ 5. In 1810, it was difficult to get weather reports quickly.

_____ 6. A weather map in the United States looks the same as one in Russia.

_____ 7. Weather forecasters use trains to help them predict the weather.

_____ 8. Weather forecasters study the weather every day except Sunday.

_____ 9. We can get weather reports quickly from Australia.

_____ 10. People around the world understand the same weather language.

Discussion Activities

Directions: *Discuss these topics as a class or in a small group.*

1. Give an example of how the weather can change the way you feel and think.
2. Tell different ways you can find out what the weather will be tomorrow.
3. How can weather change the way we live?
4. Watch a weather report on TV for three nights. Tell the class about it. Can you understand the map? What will the weather be tomorrow?

Lightning

Directions: *Read quickly. Your teacher will time you. Put your reading rate on Chart 1 in the back of this book.*

A lot of people don't worry about the weather. They just want to	13
know about it. However, there is one man who worries about one kind	26
of weather all the time. The man is Roy Sullivan. He worries about	39
lightning storms. Lightning has struck Sullivan seven times in the past	50
25 years. Sullivan is lucky he isn't dead. Lightning kills many people the	63
first time it hits them. In the United States, lightning kills more than 200	77
people every year. Lightning hurts more than 400 people every year.	88

Scientists know what lightning is. It is a big spark of electricity that	101
goes from the sky down to the earth. Lightning storms happen most	113
often in the spring and summer. It is during these times that lightning	126
hits most people. Lightning happens in thunderstorms. Thunder makes	135
the noise. Lightning makes the light.	141

Figure 29   Lightning

Scientists can't always save people from lightning. However, they   150
can tell us what to do. Here are some things to do so lightning won't hit   166
you. When a thunderstorm starts, get inside a house, a large building,   178
or a car. Never get under a tree that is standing alone in an open place.   194
Tall things that stand up from the earth bring lightning to them.   206

Here are some other things to do in a thunderstorm. Never swim   218
or stay in a boat during a thunderstorm. Lightning goes easily through   230
water and can find you. Stay off of metal things. Metal things bring   243
lightning to them. Get off of and away from motorcycles and bicycles   255
when they are out in the open. If there is no time to get to a safe place,   273
get down in a low spot. Stay there until the storm is over. It is better to   290
get wet than to let lightning hit you. Ask Roy Sullivan.   301

READING SKILLS EXERCISES

Reading to Find Information

Directions: *Read the question. Then move your eyes quickly over the paragraph that follows it. It is not necessary to read every word carefully. Just look for the answer to the question. Put a line under the answer. Work quickly.*

How many people does lightning kill every year?

A lot of people don't worry about the weather. They just want to know about it. However, there is one man who worries about one kind of weather all the time. The man is Roy Sullivan. He worries about lightning storms. Why? Lightning has struck Sullivan seven times in the past 25 years. Sullivan is lucky he isn't dead. Lightning kills many people the first time it hits them. In the United States lightning kills more than 200 people every year. Lightning hurts more than 400 people every year.

Reading to Find the Main Idea

Directions: *Read the 3 titles. Then read the paragraph. Choose the title that is best for the whole paragraph.*

a. Lightning Can Hurt People
b. Scientists Study Lightning
c. How to Save Yourself from Lightning

Lightning is dangerous to people, and scientists can't always save people from lightning. However, they can tell us what to do. Here are some things to do so lightning won't hit you. When a thunderstorm starts, get inside a house, a large building, or a car. Never get under a tree that is standing alone in an open place. Tall things that stand up from the earth bring lightning to them.

Using the Context

Directions: *You don't always need to know all the words in a story. You can still understand the ideas. Read the following paragraph or paragraphs. Don't worry about the blanks at first. Answer the true/false questions for all paragraphs. Then go back and fill in the blanks, choosing a word from the following list.*

Scientists know what lightning is. It is a _____ spark of electricity
                                                    1
that goes from the sky down to the earth. Lightning storms happen most often
in the spring and summer. It is during these times that lightning ____ _____
                                                                          2
most people. Lightning _____ in thunderstorms. Thunder makes the
                              3
noise. Lightning makes the light.

_____ Lightning happens more in July than in September.

Here are some other things to do in a thunderstorm. Never swim or stay in
a _____ during a thunderstorm. Lightning goes easily through water
        1
and can find you. Stay off of _____ things. Metal things pull lightning
                                      2
toward them. Get off of and away from motorcycles and _____ when
                                                                3
they are out in the open. If there is no time to get to a safe place, get down in a
low spot. Stay there until the _____ is over. It is better to get wet than
                                      4
to let lightning hit you. Ask Roy Sullivan.

_____ It is good to be on a high spot during a thunderstorm.

metal	strikes
boat	happens
storm	large
bicycles	

Timed Reading

Directions: *Read the timed reading again. Your teacher will time your reading. Put your reading rate on Chart 2 in the back of this book.*

Timed Reading Comprehension Check

Directions: 1. *Answer all the questions about the timed reading.*

2. *Go back to the timed reading and check your answers. Put a line under the answer in the timed reading. In the blank, write the line number where you found the answer in the timed reading.*

3. *When you have finished, your teacher may ask you to talk about the answers in a small group. In your group, try to agree on the answers, and then report back to the class.*

Line Number	Answer	True/False:
_____	_____	1. We need to worry about all kinds of weather.
_____	_____	2. Lightning can hit animals.
_____	_____	3. Lightning doesn't hit trees.
_____	_____	4. Scientists don't know where lightning will hit.
_____	_____	5. Roy Sullivan is a. not careful. b. lucky. c. not afraid.

Directions: *Choose one word from the list to put in each blank.*

predict	special
together	international
plan	storms

1. Lightning and thunder happen _____ in thunderstorms.

2. People from all countries worry about lighting. This worry is

    _____.

3. Roy Sullivan has a _____ problem with lightning.

4. People should _____ not to stand under trees in future lightning

    _____.

5. It is difficult to _____ where lightning will hit.

What Happens When You Sleep?

Directions: *Your teacher may use this as a timed reading in class or let you read it by yourself outside of class.*

Many people think that nothing happens when they sleep. Doctors 10
have studied sleep for many years. They think that a lot happens when 23
people sleep. 25

Doctors say that people have five kinds, or stages, of sleep. People 37
may go through each stage about every 90 minutes. 46

During the first two stages, you sleep lightly. If someone calls you 58
or puts his or her hand on you, you wake up quickly. Your body rests 73
quietly. You breathe more slowly than when you are awake. Your heart 85
beats slowly. 87

During stages three and four, you sleep deeply. If someone puts his 99
or her hand on you, you don't wake up. Your heart beats more slowly 113
than in stages one and two. You don't hear sounds. Lights don't wake 126
you up. 128

The last stage of sleep is called REM (Rapid Eye Movement). 139
During REM sleep, you breathe faster, and your heart beats faster than 151
in stages one through four. Your eyes move under your eyelids. All of 164
this happens because you are dreaming. 170

Doctors say that everyone dreams. Some dreams are short; some 180
are long. Some people are good at remembering their dreams; others 191
forget theirs. 193

Some people need more sleep than other people do. Some people 204
get rest with only 4 or 5 hours of sleep a night. Others may need 12 220
hours of sleep. Americans worry a lot about sleep. They spend at least 233
25 million dollars a year on sleeping pills. Doctors say this is a bad idea. 248
After you use sleeping pills for about 14 days, they don't help you 261
anymore. Some sleeping pills won't let you go into sleep stage four; 273
others won't let you go into REM sleep. So you don't get a good night's 288
sleep with sleeping pills. They may be dangerous. 296

What can you do to help yourself sleep? Drink a glass of warm 309
milk. Don't drink coffee or alcohol. Don't eat a lot of food before 322
bedtime. Don't exercise before bedtime. Don't lie in bed and worry 333
about your problems. 336

Why do we need sleep? Is it bad for you if you don't sleep? Doctors 351
say you won't be sick, but you will be sleepy. 361

Comprehension Check

Directions: *Read each sentence. Write T if it is true. Write F if it is false. Do not look back in the story.*

_____ 1. Nothing happens when you sleep.

_____ 2. People have four stages of sleep.

_____ 3. During the first two stages, you sleep lightly.

_____ 4. During stages three and four, lights and sounds don't bother you.

_____ 5. During REM sleep, your heartbeat and breathing slow down.

_____ 6. You dream during REM sleep.

_____ 7. Some people don't dream.

_____ 8. If you use sleeping pills for a long time, they don't help you.

_____ 9. You get a good night's sleep with sleeping pills.

_____ 10. Everyone should have at least eight hours sleep every night.

chapter 7 _____

The Calendar

Introduction

Directions: *Talk about these questions before you read the story.*

How many months are in the calendar?
Tell or write the names of the months.
How many days are in each month?
What is the shortest month? How many days does it have?

Directions: *Read the story quickly. Try to guess the meaning of new words. Don't use your dictionary.*

It is easy to understand the calendar we use today. It was not always so easy. People had to try for thousands of years before they knew how to put together days, weeks, months, and years.

More than 2,000 years ago, scientists in Egypt made a calendar. There were 10 days in a week, three weeks in a month, and 12 months in a year. This calendar showed a way to count weeks and months, but it was not scientific.

It does not matter how many days are in a week, or in a month; any number can be used. No one, however, can decide how long a day or a year should be. A day is the exact length of time it takes the earth to turn around one time. A year is the length of time the earth takes to travel around the sun one time. The Egyptians did not think about these scientific facts. For them, 12 of their 30-day months made a year, but 360 days do not make a full year.

What did they do about this problem? They made a five-day holiday at the end of each year. But even adding five holidays did not make the Egyptians' yearly calendar right. It takes the earth a little more than 365 days to travel around the sun. To be exact, it takes 365 days, 5 hours, 48 minutes, and 46 seconds. For a long time people did not add these extra hours and minutes and seconds.

It was like using a watch that runs slow. The Egyptian calendar was slower than the exact sun year. In four years, it was about a day behind; in forty years the calendar was 10 days (a full Egyptian week) behind the sun.

Many years later in Rome, Julius Caesar tried to fix the calendar. He thought that a year should be 365 days and 6 hours long. He added an extra day every four years. The year with an extra day is called *leap year*. The year is really 365 days, 5 hours, 48 minutes and 46 seconds long. Julius Caesar's calendar was almost twelve minutes too fast. Twelve minutes is not much, but by the year 1582 scientists showed that the calendar was about 10 days faster than the sun. Pope Gregory VII wanted to make a better plan.

It was easy to take 10 days away from the calendar. This made it right with the sun again. There was still a problem: how to keep the calendar right in the future, year after year.

Scientists tried one way, and then they tried another. Finally, they decided to continue to have every fourth year as a leap year. Then they solved the problem of the calendar going too fast. They made a plan to take out three days every 400 years. A year ending in 00 is not a leap year unless it can be divided evenly by 400. The year 1600 was a leap year, but 1700, 1800, and 1900 were not. The year 2000 will be a leap year.

This is the plan we use now. Our calendar, named for Pope Gregory, is called the Gregorian Calendar. It is not quite exact. It is 26 seconds fast each year by sun time. Our calendar will not be fast by a whole day for at least 3,000 years.

Check Your Guess

Directions: *You guessed the meaning of these words from this story. Circle the letter beside the answer that gives the same idea as the new word.*

1. No one can <u>decide</u> how long a day or year should be.
   a. make
   b. choose
   c. write

2. They made a five-day <u>holiday</u> at the end of the year.
   a. work
   b. birthday
   c. vacation

3. The year with an <u>extra</u> day is called leap year.
   a. another
   b. not needed
   c. vacation

4. Julius Caesar tried to <u>fix</u> the calendar.
   a. make it right
   b. make it new
   c. make it interesting

5. They <u>solved</u> the problem of the calendar going too fast.
   a. found the answer
   b. worked on
   c. made

6. Our calendar will not be fast by a <u>whole</u> day for at least 3,000 years.
   a. part
   b. all
   c. some

Comprehension Exercises

Part 1: *You can find the answers to these questions in the story. You may look back to find an answer if you don't remember.*

1. When did Egyptian scientists make a calendar?

2. How long was the Egyptian year?

3. How many weeks were in a month on the Egyptian calendar?

4. What is the name of the year that has an extra day?

5. What is the name of the calendar we use now?

Part 2: *You may not find the answers to these questions in the story, but you can answer the questions if you understand the ideas.*

1. What is a scientific calendar?

2. Explain how the Gregorian Calendar works.

3. What is a day? What is a year?

Comprehension Check

Directions: *Read each sentence. Write T if it is true. Write F if it is false. Do not look back in the story.*

_____ 1. There were seven days in a week on the Egyptian calendar.

_____ 2. Egyptians added a five-day holiday at the end of their year, and this made their year right.

_____ 3. It takes the earth 365 days, 5 hours, 48 minutes, and 46 seconds to travel around the sun one time.

_____ 4. Julius Caesar's calendar had a leap year every four years.

_____ 5. The Gregorian Calendar is exact.

_____ 6. The calendar we use now was named for Pope Gregory VII.

_____ 7. The Gregorian Calendar has a leap year every four years.

_____ 8. The Gregorian Calendar will be fast a whole day in about 3,000 years.

_____ 9. Julius Caesar's calendar was too slow.

_____ 10. The Gregorian Calendar is too slow.

Discussion Activities

Directions: *Discuss these topics as a class or in a small group.*

1. What are the seasons of the year?

2. Tell the class when your birthday is.

3. Discuss the difference between the Arabic calendar and the Gregorian Calendar. Do you know any other different calendars?

4. When did your country begin to use the Gregorian Calendar? What changes were necessary to begin to use it?

5. Which of the following years are leap years?
    a. 1900
    b. 1988
    c. 2000
    d. 2100

TIMED READING

Solstice

Directions: *Read quickly. Your teacher will time you. Put your reading rate on Chart 1 in the back of this book.*

On either June 21 or June 22, depending on the year, the northern	13
part of earth faces most directly to the sun. It is the longest day of the	29
year. We call this day the *summer solstice*. In Denver, Colorado, there are	42
15 hours of sunshine from dawn in the morning to sunset at night. At	56
the North Pole on this day the sun shines 24 hours.	67
The summer solstice is not a very important day in modern times.	79
It was different for people a long time ago. Before people had modern	92
calendars, they kept time by the sun. They thought the sun was a god.	106
Some examples of sun gods were: Ra (Egyptian), Helios (Greek), Apollo	117
(Greek and Roman), Sol (Roman), Kon-tiki (Polynesian), Mithias	125

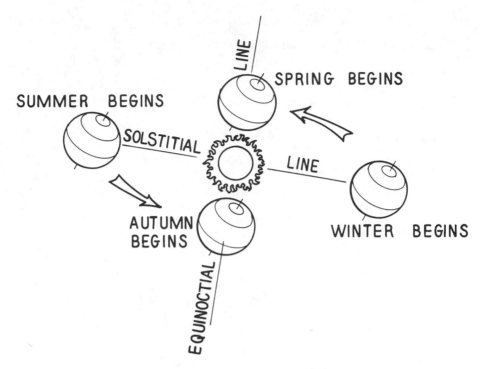

Figure 30   Equinoxes and solstices

(Persian) and Saule (Baltic). In North and South America, the Anasazi   136
Indians of New Mexico, the Inca Indians of Peru and the Aztec Indians   149
of Mexico had sun gods. The summer solstice was a very important day   162
for these people.   165

In the southern part of England there is a circle of large stones.   178
Some of the stones are 30 feet high and weigh about 60,000 pounds. This   192
circle of stones is called Stonehenge. Stonehenge was built by people   203
who lived in England about 4,000 years ago. These people did not leave   216
any writing to help us learn about how they lived. Scientists have   228
learned something about them from Stonehenge. Scientists think that   237
Stonehenge was a calendar because of the way the stones were placed.   249
The stones point to the most northerly place where the sun comes up   262
during the year. The line in the picture of Stonehenge shows where the   275
sun rises around June 21 or 22. People were able to know the seasons by   290
the way the sun shone on the stones. Today people still go to   303
Stonehenge to watch the sun on the summer solstice. They want to see   316
how the oldest and largest calendar works.   323

Most people around the world have fun outside on the longest day   335
of the year. For example, for more than 25 years, two teams have played   349
the Midnight Sun baseball game in Fairbanks, Alaska. Sometimes they   359
play until 3 A.M. Can you guess why?   367

DIRECTION
OF SUNRISE
ON SUMMER
SOLSTICE

■ ◨ STONES IN POSITION
▱ STONE MISSING OR FALLEN

Figure 31 Stonehenge today

READING SKILLS EXERCISES

Reading to Find Information

Directions: *Read the question. Then move your eyes over the paragraph that follows it. It is not necessary to read every word carefully. Just look for the answer to the question. Put a line under the answer. Work quickly.*

How long ago did Stonehenge people live?

In the southern part of England there is a circle of large stones. Some of the stones are 30 feet high and weigh about 60,000 pounds. This circle of stones is called Stonehenge. Stonehenge was built by people who lived in England about 4,000 years ago. These people did not leave any writing to help us learn about how they lived.

What was Stonehenge?

Scientists have learned something about these people from Stonehenge. Scientists think that Stonehenge was a calendar because of the way the stones were placed. The stones point to the most northerly place where the sun comes up during the year. The line in the picture of Stonehenge shows where the sun rises on June 21 or 22. People were able to know the seasons by the way the sun shone on the stones.

How many years has the Midnight Sun baseball game been played?

Most people around the world have fun outside on the longest day of the year. For example, for more than 25 years, two teams have played the Midnight Sun baseball game in Fairbanks, Alaska. Sometimes they play until 3 A.M. Can you guess why?

Reading to Find the Main Idea

Directions: *Read the three titles. Then read the paragraph. Choose the title that is best for the whole paragraph.*

  a. The Longest Day of the Year
  b. Twenty-four Hours of Sunshine at the North Pole
  c. Why We Have a Summer Solstice

On June 21 or 22, the northern part of the earth faces most directly to the sun. It is the longest day of the year. We call this day the *summer solstice*. In Denver, Colorado, there are 15 hours of sunshine from dawn in the morning to sunset at night. At the North Pole on this day the sun shines 24 hours.

  a. The Incas' Sun God
  b. In the Andes Mountains with the Inca Indians
  c. Why the Solstice was Important to the Incas

The Incas did not eat or make fires for three days before the solstice. Their god, Inti, came on that day. All the Indians went to the Andes Mountains. They shouted and made a big noise when the sun came up.

a. How the Aztecs Worshipped Their Sun God
b. The King of Mexico
c. Why People Were Killed in Mexico

For one year, an average man in Mexico lived like a king. The Aztecs gave him all the food and drink he wanted and beautiful clothes. Then on June 21, on the solstice, they killed him and gave his blood to their sun god, Tanatuck.

Using the Context

Directions: *You don't always need to know all of the words in a story. You can still understand the ideas. Read the following paragraph or paragraphs. Don't worry about the blanks at first. Answer the true/false questions for all paragraphs. Then go back and fill in the blanks, choosing a word from the following list.*

Some people who _____ before calendars kept time by the sun.
1
Others kept time by the moon. They saw that the moon was _____ full.
2
Then it changed from a small moon to a half moon to a full moon over a period of time. They counted these _____ like our months, but one moon
3
period was less than a _____. The American Indians kept time
4
_____ the moon. They might have said, "I haven't seen you for many
5
moons."

_____ The moon calendar was exact.

month	minute
added	calendar
lived	periods
by	sometimes
always	from

Timed Reading

Directions: *Read the timed reading again. Your teacher will time your reading. Put your reading rate on Chart 2 in the back of this book.*

Timed Reading Comprehension Check

Directions:
1. *Answer all the questions about the timed reading.*
2. *Go back to the timed reading and check your answers. Put a line under the answer in the timed reading. In the blank, write the line number where you found the answer in the timed reading.*
3. *When you have finished, your teacher may ask you to talk about the answers in a small group. In your group try to agree on the answers, and then report back to the class.*

Line
Number   *Answer*

_____   _____   1. Which of the following are not examples of sun gods?
                    a. Kon-tiki   d. Apollo
                    b. Anasazi   e. All of the above
                    c. Ra

                    True/False

_____   _____   2. We know a lot about Stonehenge people.

_____   _____   3. Stonehenge people were probably intelligent.

_____   _____   4. Stonehenge people were probably strong.

_____   _____   5. Mexico has more hours of sunshine on June 21 than England.

Directions: *Choose one word from the list to put in each blank.*

decided   solve
whole   holiday
fix   extra

1. At the North Pole on the solstice, the sun shines for a _____ day.

2. There were too many problems on the mathematics test. I didn't have time to _____ them all.

3. My TV doesn't work. I need to get someone to _____ it.

4. I didn't have to work on Monday. It was a _____.

5. Do you have an _____ pencil that I can use?

6. I looked at all the food on the menu. Finally I _____ to have a hamburger.

The Harmonic Convergence

Directions: *Your teacher may use this as a timed reading in class or let you read it by yourself outside of class.*

Astronomers are scientists who watch and study the sun, planets,	10
moons, and stars in the universe. They study about unusual things that	22
happen in the sky. These unusual things may happen hundreds or	33
thousands of years apart. Astronomers are happy to be living when	44
something very unusual happens so they can see it.	53
Halley's comet moves through the sky. It travels near enough to	64
the earth so that we can see it only once every 76 years. The last time we	81
saw it was in 1986. We will not see it again until about 2062.	95
The earth travels around the sun. The moon travels around the	106
earth. About every 22 years the earth and the moon are in a straight line	121
with the sun. Scientists call this *syzygy*.	128
On August 15, 1987, something happened in the universe that	138
happens only once every 5,125 years. The planets and stars were lined	150
up in the shape of a pyramid or triangle. Astronomers called this	162
convergence. They thought it was interesting, but it was just an accident.	174
Astronomers do not think convergence can change our lives on earth.	185
Astrologers are not scientists; they are people who like to tell the	197
future by the planets and stars. They think the way the planets and stars	211
move can change our lives. Astrologers think the convergence was the	222
beginning of a very important time for people on earth. They think this	235
will be a time without wars and problems. It will be a time of peace and	251
harmony on earth. They called it the *harmonic convergence*.	260
There is another reason August 15, 1987, was an important date.	271
The Aztec and Mayan Indians lived in Mexico and South America from	283
300 to 900 A.D. Around 800 A.D., the Indians made one of the first	297
calendars; it had symbols cut in stone. This calendar is difficult for us to	311
understand today, but one astrologer has an idea. He thinks the Mayan	323
calendar begins in 843 A.D. and ended in 1987. It has 22 time periods of	338
52 years each. The Mayans thought that something important would	348
happen on earth at the end of each time period. August 15, 1987, was	362
the end of the Mayan calendar. People think something important will	373
happen now, and it will be something good.	381

The convergence and the end of the Mayan calendar happened at the same time. Thousands of people got together at sunrise on August 15, 1987, to see this new time begin. They gathered at famous places around the world: Mount Shasta in California, Chaco Canyon in New Mexico, Machu Picchu in Peru, the Pyramid of the Sun in Mexico, Stonehenge in England, and the pyramids in Egypt.

392
404
417
428
440
448

Was this the beginning of a time of peace and harmony on earth? We will have to wait and see.

461
468

Comprehension Questions

Directions: *Read each sentence. Write T if it is true. Write F if it is false. Do not look back in the story.*

_____   1.   Astronomers and astrologers study different things about the universe.

_____   2.   Halley's Comet comes by the earth every 22 years.

_____   3.   Halley's Comet came by the earth around 1919.

_____   4.   The sun, earth, and moon are sometimes in a straight line.

_____   5.   The Mayan calendar started in 300 A.D.

_____   6.   The Mayan calendar is easy to read.

_____   7.   Some people believe a good, peaceful period is beginning for everyone.

_____   8.   Machu Picchu is in Mexico.

_____   9.   A syzygy happens every 10 years.

_____   10.   Most people celebrate a syzygy.

chapter 8 _____

The Pony Express

Introduction

Directions: *Talk about these questions before you read the story.*

Who do you send mail to?

What do you have to do to send a letter?

How long does it usually take to get there?

How much does it cost?

How does the letter travel?

Directions: *Read the story quickly. Try to guess the meaning of new words. Don't use your dictionary.*

The U.S. Postal Service was not always big and fast like it is now. It grew along with the country. There are many interesting stories in its history, but the most interesting is the story of the Pony Express.

In 1860, not many people lived in the western part of the United States. People lived in the eastern part as far as the Mississippi River. People also lived in California, but in between the country was mostly empty. There were some

Figure 32 Pony Express rider

Indians and wild animals, mountains and deserts, but no farms or cities or roads. There were no railroads across the West at this time. It was very difficult and dangerous to cross this empty land. A letter might take months to go from California to the East, or it might never get there at all.

Many people wanted to keep California closely tied to the eastern United States. In 1860, William Russell began the Pony Express to send the mail from San Francisco, California, to St. Joseph, Missouri. From Missouri, the mail went by train to the East.

Russell bought 400 fast horses and got 80 men to ride them. He built 80 stations to keep the horses along the way and got 200 men to take care of the stations and horses. The stations were 25 to 30 miles apart. At every station the rider changed horses. After three to five stations, the riders changed. In this way, the horses and riders could go as fast as possible over difficult land.

Riders from the western team started in San Francisco. The eastern team started from St. Joseph, Missouri, at the same time. They rode fast to see which team could get to Bear River, Wyoming first. There they changed bags of mail and turned back again the way they had come. The riders on fast horses took the mail almost 2,000 miles in ten days.

They rode through snow and rain, mountains, wild animals and many dangers. Two riders were killed while carrying the mail.

The Pony Express carried the mail of the West for only 18 months. Workers finished the railroad across the West at the end of 1861. The Pony Express was

Figure 33 Pony Express route

not needed anymore. The mail went by train. There are many stories, books and movies about this interesting time in American history.

Today mail is delivered every day except Sundays and holidays. The weather does not stop delivery of letters and packages. These words on the main Post Office building in New York City can be used to describe the work of the Postal Service since the days of the Pony Express:

Neither snow nor rain nor heat nor gloom of night stays these couriers from the swift completion of their appointed rounds.

—Herodotus

Check Your Guess

Directions: *You guessed the meaning of these words from this story. Circle the letter beside the answer that gives the same idea as the new word.*

1. The <u>riders</u> on fast horses took the mail almost 2,000 miles in 10 days.

    a. to travel

    b. a person who rides

    c. a trip

2. He built 80 <u>stations</u> to keep the horses along the way and got 200 men to take care of the stations and horses.
   a. a building that is a regular stopping place for travelers
   b. a place to buy gas
   c. a police station

3. There were some <u>Indians</u> and wild animals, mountains and deserts, but no farms or cities or roads.
   a. a state in the United States
   b. a country in Asia
   c. first people in North and South America

4. Riders from the western <u>team</u> started in San Francisco.
   a. state
   b. people who work together as a group
   c. United States

5. At Bear River, Wyoming, the two teams changed bags of <u>mail</u> and turned back again the way they had come.
   a. letters and packages
   b. letters
   c. packages

Comprehension Exercises

Part 1: *You can find the answers to these questions in the story. You may look back to find an answer if you don't remember.*

1. When did the Pony Express begin?

2. Where did the Pony Express riders travel?

3. How many men were there? How many horses? How many stations?

4. Where did the two teams meet?

5. How long did the Pony Express last?

Part 2: *You may not find the answers to these questions in the story, but you can answer the questions if you understand the ideas.*

1. What was dangerous about the job of Pony Express rider?

2. What was dangerous about the job of station keeper?

3. How long did it take to send a letter from California to the East before the Pony Express? By Pony Express?

4. Why do you think it was important to have a Postal Service between California and the eastern United States in 1860?

5. Why do you think there are many stories and movies about this time in history?

Comprehension Check

Directions: *Read each sentence. Write T if it is true. Write F if it is false. Do not look back in the story.*

_____ 1. In 1860 there were roads between California and Missouri.

_____ 2. There were only a few riders and horses at the beginning of the Pony Express.

_____ 3. Pony Express riders from California rode to Bear River, Wyoming, and back to California.

_____ 4. Pony Express riders changed horses often.

_____ 5. William Russell started the Pony Express to make money.

_____ 6. The two teams met in St. Joseph, Missouri.

_____ 7. Some Pony Express riders were killed.

_____ 8. Riders took the mail 2,000 miles in 10 days.

_____ 9. The Pony Express carried the mail for many years.

_____ 10. The Pony Express stopped because there was a better way to take the mail.

Discussion Activities

Directions: *Discuss these topics as a class or in a small group.*

1. Call or visit a Post Office. Find out how much it costs to send a 1-ounce letter or a 1-pound package to Venezuela, Mexico, California, and Japan. Besides buying a stamp, what do you have to do to send a package to another country? How does your family send mail to you?

2. Bring stamps from your country to show the class. Bring any other interesting stamp showing an important person, place, or thing.

3. What do you do to make sure mail arrives in your country? Is the mail in your country dependable?

4. At the Post Office, learn about certified mail, express mail, registered mail, telegrams, and FAX services. Tell the class how each of these services is different from the others.

TIMED READING

Stamps

Directions: *Read quickly. Your teacher will time you. Put your reading rate on Chart 1 in the back of this book.*

The modern U.S. Postal Service moves more than 360 million	10
pieces of mail every day. That is about two pieces of mail every day for	25
every man, woman, and child in the United States. The Postal Service	37
uses machines, computers, and approximately 660,000 people to move	46
the mail. You can send a letter from New York to Los Angeles in three or	62
four days.	64
The U.S. Postal Service sells more than 27 billion stamps every	75
year. Some people use these stamps to mail letters. Other people save or	88
collect the stamps because the stamps are beautiful and interesting.	98
These people are stamp collectors.	103
The Postal Service often decides to make new stamps. They know	114
that the stamps will carry mail all over the world. They choose pictures	127
that tell about the country and people. Every stamp is a picture that has	141
a story to tell. Stamps bring pictures from the whole world into your	154
home.	155
On stamps you meet famous people of history: Napoleon,	164
Cleopatra, Shakespeare, Alexander the Great, Julius Caesar and	172

OFFICIAL U.S. FIRST DAY COVERS

Figure 34 First day cover

Magellan. Postage stamps show you pictures of famous ships, trains,   182
airplanes and submarines. Stamps show copies of more famous   191
paintings than you will find in any art museum. In fact, you can find a   206
picture of just about any important person, place or thing in the world   219
on stamps.   221

When a new stamp is made, the Postal Service decides where the   233
stamp will be sold first. They usually choose a certain city because the   246
picture on the stamp has something to do with that city. Several weeks   259
before the stamp is ready, the Postal Service tells about it in newspapers   272
and stamp collectors' magazines. Anyone can buy the new stamp on the   284
first day it is sold. The stamps that are sold on their first day are called   300
first day covers.   303

You can get a first day cover. Get an envelope with your name and   317
address on it and enough money for the stamp. Then send it to the   331
Postmaster in the city where the stamp will be sold first. On the first day,   346
the Postmaster will put the new stamp on your envelope and send it to   360
you. People think first day covers may be worth a lot of money in the   375
future.   376

A stamp may be worth a lot of money if there are only a few like it   393
in the world. In 1847, the governor of the island of Mauritius wanted to   407
have some stamps made for his island. He wanted them to be like   420
stamps from England. An artist did a good job of copying an English   433
stamp, but he made a mistake. He didn't put on the words *Post Paid*—he   448
put *Post Office*. Only about 30 stamps were sold before he saw the   461
mistake and changed it. Those 30 stamps are now worth a lot of money.   475
It is difficult to find them. One stamp collector paid $35,000 for an   488
envelope with two of these stamps on it.   496

Save all the different and interesting stamps you can find. One of   508
them may be worth a lot of money someday.   517

READING SKILLS EXERCISES

Reading to Find Information

Directions: *Read the question. Then move your eyes over the paragraph that follows it. It is not necessary to read every word carefully. Just look for the answer to the question. Put a line under the answer. Work quickly.*

What do we call someone who saves stamps?

The U.S. Postal Service sells more than 27 billion stamps every year. Some people use these stamps to mail letters. Other people save or collect the stamps because the stamps are beautiful and interesting. These people are stamp collectors.

How many people work for the Postal Service?

The modern U.S. Postal Service moves more than 360 million pieces of mail every day. That is about two pieces of mail every day for every man, woman, and child in the United States. The Postal Service uses machines, computers, and approximately 660,000 people to move the mail. You can send a letter from New York to Los Angeles in three or four days.

Reading to Find the Main Idea

Directions: *Read the three titles. Then read the paragraph. Choose the title that is best for the whole paragraph.*

a. When to Send for a First Day Cover

b. Where to Get a First Day Cover
c. How to Get a First Day Cover

You can get a first day cover. Get an envelope with your name and address on it and enough money for the stamp. Then send it to the Postmaster in the city where the stamp will be sold. On the first day, the Postmaster will put a new stamp on your envelope and send it to you. People think first day covers may be worth a lot of money in the future.

a. What You Can Find on Stamps
b. Famous People on Stamps
c. Famous Paintings on Stamps

On stamps you meet famous people of history: Napoleon, Cleopatra, Shakespeare, Alexander the Great, Julius Caesar and Magellan. Postage stamps show you pictures of famous ships, trains, airplanes and submarines. Stamps show copies of more famous paintings than you will find in any art museum. In fact, you can find a picture of just about any important person, place, or thing in the world on stamps.

Using the Context

Directions: *You don't always need to know all of the words in a story. You can still understand the ideas. Read the following paragraph or paragraphs. Don't worry about the blanks at first. Answer the true/false questions for all paragraphs. Then go back and fill in the blanks, choosing a word from the following list.*

A stamp may be worth a lot of money if there are only a few like it in the world. In 1847, the governor of the island of Mauritius wanted to have some stamps made for his _____. He wanted them to be like stamps from England. An artist did a good job of copying an _____ stamp, but he

₁

₂

made a mistake. He didn't put on the words *Post Paid*—he put *Post Office*. Only about 30 stamps were _____ before he saw the mistake and changed

₃

it. Those 30 stamps are now worth a lot of money. It is difficult to find them. One stamp collector paid $35,000 for an _____ with two of these stamps on

₄

it.

_____ A stamp is worth more money if there are a lot of stamps like it in the world.

A young boy in England found some old boxes in the _____ in his house. They were boxes of things that had belonged to his grandfather. In the boxes he _____ some old letters. On the letters were some interesting stamps. He had never seen stamps like them before. He took the stamps to a _____ and sold them for 25¢ each. One of those stamps was later sold for $50,000. There are _____ two like it in the world.

_____It is difficult to know if a stamp is worth a lot of money.

found	envelope
sold	basement
English	island
only	shop

Timed Reading

Directions: *Read the timed reading again. Your teacher will time your reading. Put your reading rate on Chart 2 in the back of this book.*

Timed Reading Comprehension Check

Directions: *1. Answer all the questions about the timed reading.*

2. Go back to the timed reading and check your answers. Put a line under the answer in the timed reading. In the blank, write the line number where you found the answer in the timed reading.

3. When you have finished, your teacher may ask you to talk about the answers in a small group. In your group, try to agree on the answers and then report back to the class.

Line Number	Answer	True/False:
_____	_____	1. It takes about a week for a letter to go from New York to San Francisco.
_____	_____	2. You can probably find a stamp with a picture of astronauts on it.
_____	_____	3. A stamp about the Grand Canyon would probably be sold first in California.
_____	_____	4. First day covers are sold to stamp collectors first.
_____	_____	5. If there is a mistake on a stamp, it is worth more money.

Directions: *Choose one word from the list to put in each blank.*

riders	station
Indians	mail
	team

1. The Postal Service moves two pieces of _____ every day for every man, woman and child in the United States.

2. The _____ were the first people who lived in the western United States.

3. The Pony Express _____ changed horses at the _____.

4. My favorite _____ won the football game last week.

Across

3. A person who studies science
5. Think about what to do in the future
8. Repair something
11. Small bits of water
12. This shows east, west, north, and south
13. A key in a box in the corner of an illustration
15. Describing all nations together
18. Something in space that goes around the sun and reflects light
20. E, W, N, S
21. It can be done
22. Think about all the possibilities and then choose one
23. Very small pieces of rock in the desert
24. The sun and all the planets that go around it
27. Go on a trip

Down

1. Send light back
2. Show
3. A machine that takes astronauts into space
4. What a radio receives
6. Another
7. Different; for just one person or thing
9. Tell what will happen in the future
10. Small drops of water in the air, like a cloud
14. To cut into pieces
16. The same
17. A round hole on the moon
19. a, b, c, d, e, etc.
24. Find the answer to a problem
25. Bad weather
26. There's nothing in it!

chapter 9 _____

History of Money in the United States

Introduction

Directions: *Talk about these questions before you read the story.*

Do you have any U.S. money in your pocket?

Show the class some coins and bills.

Bring money from your country to class. Tell the class what it is worth compared to the dollar.

What is the unit of money called in some other countries?

What is it worth compared to the dollar?

Directions: *Read the story quickly. Try to guess the meaning of new words. Don't use your dictionary.*

Thousands of years ago, people used many different kinds of money. Sometimes they paid for food or clothes with animals as money. Sometimes they used food as money to buy things. Later, people began to use metal coins to buy things. They used silver, gold, and copper for money. At that time, silver was more important than gold. People often used silver as money.

Figure 35 What has been money? Just about everything.

Americans used many other kinds of money before they had dollars and cents. The first people who came to this country traded with the Indians they found here. The Algonquin Indians in the northeastern United States used shells for money and called it *wampum*. They also used beads, blankets, and animal furs for money. There were some problems when people used these

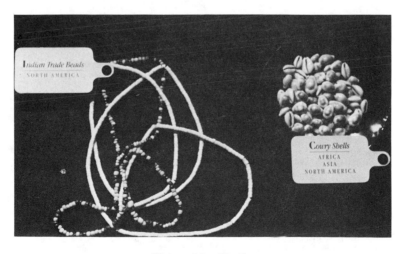

Figure 36 Shells

things for money. They were large and heavy; people couldn't carry them in their pockets. It was difficult to know how many beads or shells they needed to buy something.

More people came to America from many different countries. They brought louis d'ors from France, guineas from England, pistoles from Spain, and thalers from Germany. People used these coins in America too. There were problems when they used only coins. Sometimes they needed a lot of coins to buy something. A large number of coins is very heavy. It is difficult to find a safe place to keep a large number of coins.

People began to make their own paper money, or currency. Anyone could print* money, and many people did. Banks, insurance companies, stores, and schools printed many different kinds of paper money. The money had different values; that is, it had a different meaning in different places. The same money might have more value in Massachusetts than it did in New York.

In 1863, President Lincoln made a law. This law said that only the United States government could print money. The law gave us the kind of money we have today. At that time, people could take their money to banks. At the banks they could get a certain amount of silver in exchange for the money. In 1873, the banks began to give gold for paper money. The idea worked if too many people did not go to the banks at the same time. Banks did not always have enough gold. The government stopped this about 50 years ago. We can no longer go to banks and get gold for our money. The government will not exchange anything for paper money.

The value of money we use today is not the same as animals or food. It is not the same as an amount of silver, gold, or copper. The way people used money a long time ago may have been easier than it is today. They knew what it meant. Today the money in our pockets means different things at different times.

Check Your Guess

Directions: *You guessed the meaning of these words from this story. Circle the letter beside the answer that gives the same idea as the new word. Do not use a dictionary.*

1. The first people who came to this country used shells for money like the Indians did. Indians called this money *wampum*. They also used beads, blankets, and animal furs for money.

   a. furs

   b. shells

   c. blankets

*print—to put letters, numbers or pictures onto paper

2. The money had different <u>values</u>; that is, it had a different meaning in different places.
   a. size
   b. weight
   c. meaning

3. At the banks they could get a <u>certain</u> amount of silver in exchange for the money. In 1873, the banks began to give gold for paper money.
   a. sure
   b. big
   c. small

4. At the banks they could get a certain amount of silver in <u>exchange</u> for the money. In 1873, the banks began to give gold for paper money.
   a. part
   b. trade
   c. hand

5. In 1873, the banks began to give gold for paper money. The idea <u>worked</u> if too many people did not go to the banks at the same time. Banks did not always have enough money.
   a. ended
   b. began
   c. did well

6. People began to make their own <u>currency</u>.
   a. furs
   b. coins
   c. paper money

Comprehension Exercises

Part 1: *You can find the answers to these questions in the story. You may look back to find an answer if you don't remember.*

1. What did people use for money thousands of years ago?

2. What did the American Indians use for money?

3. Before 1863, who could print money in the United States?

4. Until 50 years ago, where could we go to get gold for our currency?

5. When did the idea of getting gold for money not work?

Part 2: *You may not find the answers to these questions in the story, but you can answer the questions if you understand the ideas.*

1. Why did people begin to use metals like gold and silver for money?

2. Can anything be used as money today in the United States?

3. Could people get gold in exchange for paper money in 1924?

4. Look at Figure 35. Name some of the things in the picture that have been money.

5. Why did people use food or clothing for money thousands of years ago?

Comprehension Check

Directions: *Read each sentence. Write T if it is true. Write F if it is false. Do not look back in the story.*

_____ 1. People did not use animals as money.

_____ 2. American Indians used shells as *wampum*.

_____ 3. In 1790, Americans used nickels, quarters, dimes, and dollars.

_____ 4. People used paper money because coins were heavy.

_____ 5. In early America, schools sometimes made their own money.

_____ 6. After 1863, only the United States government could print money.

_____ 7. In 1873, the banks began to give silver for paper money.

_____ 8. We can now get gold in exchange for paper money.

_____ 9. The banks always had enough gold to give for paper money.

_____ 10. In 1940, Americans could get gold for money.

Discussion Activities

Directions: *Discuss these topics as a class or in a small group.*

1. How is money in other countries different from money in the United States?
2. Do you carry much currency with you, or do you like to carry credit cards instead of money?
3. Show a penny, nickel, dime, quarter, half dollar, and token to the class. What other coins and bills are available? Are they difficult to find?
4. What are the names of some different credit cards? Can you show some to the class?
5. When do you need bills, coins, tokens, checks, or credit cards?

TIMED READING

Money of the Future

Directions: *Read quickly. Your teacher will time you. Put your reading rate on Chart 1 in the back of this book.*

Someday in the future we may not need to have money in our	13
pockets. Is life easier when people don't need to carry any coins or	26
currency? Is money heavy to carry? Is it safe to carry money? Maybe in	40
the future each of us will have only one small plastic credit card. We will	55
use it to buy all the things we now buy with money. We will not need	71
money to pay for things.	76
Of course we may still have some of the same problems with cards	89
that we now have with money. Sometimes we lose money. Maybe we	101
will lose the card. People steal money. Maybe someone will take the	113
card. Someone may even make a card that looks like our card. Since we	127
can't buy anything without our card, the credit card may be no better	140
than currency.	142
Is there something even easier to use than credit cards? All of us	155
have a thumbprint. No two thumbprints are the same. Maybe someday	166
the government will keep people's thumbprints with a number. No two	177
people will have the same thumbprint or number. When we want to buy	190
something, we will put our thumbs on a machine or computer. Each	212

store or business will have one. Everyone's thumbprint will be in the 224
computers. It will be very difficult to lose our thumbprint. It will be 237
difficult for someone to steal it or make one like it. 248

READING SKILLS EXERCISES

Reading to Find Information

Directions: *Read the question. Then move your eyes over the paragraph that follows it. It is not necessary to read every word carefully. Just look for the answer to the question. Put a line under the answer. Work quickly.*

How many credit cards will each of us have?

Someday in the future we may not need to have money in our pockets. Is life easier when people don't need to carry any coins or currency? Is money heavy to carry? Is it safe to carry money? Maybe in the future each of us will have only one small plastic credit card. We will use it to buy all the things we now buy with money. We will not need money to pay for things.

Reading to Find the Main Idea

Directions: *Read the three titles. Then read the paragraph. Choose the title that is best for the whole paragraph.*

a. Credit Cards Have the Same Problems as Currency
b. People Steal Both Credit Cards and Money
c. Credit Cards Will Be Better than Currency

Of course we may still have some of the same problems with cards that we now have with money. Sometimes we lose money. Maybe we will lose the card. People steal money. Maybe someone will take the card. Someone may even make a card that looks like our card. Since we can't buy anything without our card, the credit card may be no better than currency.

Using the Context

Directions: *You don't always need to know all of the words in a story. You can still understand the ideas. Read the following paragraph or paragraphs. Don't worry about the blanks at first. Answer the true/false questions for all paragraphs. Then go back and fill in the blanks, choosing a word from the following list.*

Is there something easier to use than _____? All of us have a thumbprint. No two thumbprints are the _____. Maybe someday the government will keep people's thumbprints with a number. No two _____ will have the same thumbprint or number. When we want to buy something, we will put our thumbs on a machine or computer. Each store or business will have one. Everyone's thumbprint will be int he computers. It will be very _____ to lose our thumbprint. It will be difficult for someone to _____ it or make one like it.

_____ Our thumbprints will be used in the future because they will help the government.

Many people spend too much with their credit cards because it is so easy. You see something you want. You don't have any money. You take out your credit card and buy what you want. You don't need _____. You don't even have to think about how much it costs—until the end of the month when the bill comes. _____, you must pay a lot of money and you are _____. No money? Don't worry. Just pay a little bit every month, plus 22 percent interest. Every month you pay a little bit, but when the bill comes again, you still owe almost as much. It is very difficult to finish paying a credit card bill if you only pay a little each _____.

_____ You must pay more money to the credit card company than just the amount you charged.

worried	people
month	same
money	steal
suddenly	difficult

Timed Reading

Directions: *Read the timed reading again. Your teacher will time your reading. Put your reading rate on Chart 2 in the back of this book.*

Timed Reading Comprehension Check

Directions: 1. *Answer all the questions about the timed reading.*

2. *Go back to the timed reading and check your answers. Put a line under the answer in the timed reading. In the blank, write the line number where you found the answer in the timed reading.*

3. *When you have finished, your teacher may ask you to talk about the answers in a small group. In your group, try to agree on the answers, and then report back to the class.*

Line
Number   *Answer*

_____   _____   1. Which of these statements is true?
a. There are no problems with credit cards.
b. Some people's thumbprints are the same.
c. There are some problems now with the use of money.

_____   _____   2. We all need
a. some kind of money.
b. computers.
c. credit cards.

_____   _____   3. Which sentence is not true?
a. It will be difficult to lose our thumbprint.
b. It will be difficult for someone to steal our thumbprint.
c. Everyone's thumbprint is the same.

_____   _____   4. Our thumbprint is
a. difficult to use.
b. easy to lose.
c. different from other thumbprints.
d. all of the above.

_____   _____   5. Some people use credit cards
a. now.
b. to pay for clothes.
c. to buy gas.
d. all of the above.

Directions: *Choose one word from the list to put in each blank.*

wampum   currency
value   exchange
work

1. Do you think credit cards are better than _____?

2. In the future when we want to buy something, maybe we will put our thumbprint on a computer. Maybe this idea will _____ better than credit cards.

3. What is the _____ of a thumbprint? One dollar, 10 dollars, or 100 dollars?

4. Today you can't get any gold or silver at a bank in _____ for currency.

5. Indians' money was called _____.

chapter 10 _____

Should People Marry Young?

Introduction

Directions: *Talk about these questions before you read the story.*

Are you married? If so, how old were you when you married?

Was it a good idea to marry at that age?

If you aren't married, at what age do you want to marry?

Is age important for a good marriage? Why?

Directions: *Read the story quickly. Try to guess the meaning of new words. Don't use your dictionary.*

Thirty to forty years ago, most young people in the United States planned to marry before they were 20 years old. Americans today marry later than they did before. Now the average age for men to marry is 24. The average age for women is between 21 and 22.

Is this a good idea or a bad idea? Should young people marry before age 20 or be a little older? We will talk to two people so we can hear both sides of this question. First, we will talk to Dr. Sidney Bernbaum. He is a marriage counselor. He wrote the book *How to Stay Married Longer*.

Interviewer:	Dr. Bernbaum, at what age do you think people should marry?
Dr. Bernbaum:	Generally, I think it is a good idea for people to marry at an older age. Older people are usually more grown-up. Grown-up people can take care of themselves. They can take care of the problems of marriage better too.
Interviewer:	Why should people marry later?
Dr. Bernbaum:	If two people marry later, they can finish their education and find good jobs before marriage. They can have a better marriage if they have good jobs. Older people can know more and different kinds of people. If they know more people, they can understand their husband or wife better. This helps make a happy marriage.
Interviewer:	What about children?
Dr. Bernbaum:	If two people marry later, they may not have a lot of children. That is good. There are already too many people in the world. Smaller families are better.

Next we will talk to Mr. Tom Nelson. He married when he was 20 years old. He has been married for nine years.

Interviewer:	Mr. Nelson, at what age do you think people should marry?
Mr. Nelson:	It is too bad that people marry later now. I married when I was 20, and I have been happy. I think young love is better. Young

Figure 37   Robert and Dora Knight on their wedding day, July 5, 1903

people believe in people more. Older people see many more problems. It is more difficult for them to believe in others.

Interviewer: Why should people marry young?

Mr. Nelson: Young people who marry have something to live for. They don't have time to play around with other young people. They don't go to parties and drink a lot. They get busy. They work and make a happy life.

Interviewer: What about children?

Mr. Nelson: Young people are better mothers and fathers too. Young parents can still remember what it is like to be children. They are more understanding. Young parents are stronger. I am still young enough to play with my children. I take them camping in the mountains.

If two people marry young, they have time to have all the children they want. When their children are grown-up, the parents will still be young enough to enjoy life.

It think it is a bad idea for people to marry later. This is why marriages and families have so many problems today.

Check Your Guess

Directions: *You guessed the meaning of these words from this story. Circle around the letter beside the answer that gives the same idea as the new word. Do not use a dictionary.*

1. First we will talk to Dr. Sidney Bernbaum. He is a marriage <u>counselor</u>. He wrote the book *How to Stay Married Longer.*
   a. doctor
   b. helper
   c. writer

2. Americans today marry later than they did before. Now the average age for men to marry is 24. The <u>average</u> age for women is between 21 and 22.
   a. highest
   b. lowest
   c. usual

3. <u>Interviewer</u>: What about children?
   a. a person who tells stories
   b. a person who asks questions
   c. a person who writes books

4. Older people are more <u>grown-up</u>. Grown-up people can take care of themselves. They can take care of the problems of marriage better too.

   a. not children

   b. young

   c. fat

5. I think young love is better. Young people <u>believe in</u> people more. Older people see many more problems. It is more difficult for them to believe in others.

   a. think people are bad

   b. think people are old

   c. think people are good

Comprehension Exercises

Part 1: *You can find the answers to these questions in the story. You may look back to find an answer if you don't remember.*

1. At what age did most young people marry, 30 to 40 years ago in the United States?

2. What is the average age for men and women to marry now?

3. Who are the two people interviewed in this reading?

4. Tell three reasons for marrying later.

5. Tell three reasons for marrying young.

Part 2: *You may not find the answers to these questions in the story, but you can answer the questions if you understand the ideas.*

1. Why do you think Dr. Sidney Bernbaum is a good person to speak about marriage?

2. Why is Tom Nelson a good person to speak about marrying young?

3. Tell what Dr. Bernbaum or Tom Nelson thinks:
   a. Smaller families are better.
   b. Young love is better.
   c. People should be grown-up before they marry.
   d. It is better to know more and different people.

Comprehension Check

Directions: *Read each sentence. Write T if it is true. Write F if it is false. Do not look back in the story.*

_____ 1. Most young people in the United States marry before they are 20.

_____ 2. The average age for women to marry is 24.

_____ 3. Tom Nelson wrote *How to Stay Married Longer*.

_____ 4. Dr. Bernbaum thinks people can have a better marriage if they have good jobs.

_____ 5. Tom Nelson thinks you can understand your husband or wife better if you know more people.

_____ 6. Tom Nelson has been married two years.

_____ 7. Dr. Bernbaum thinks young love is better.

_____ 8. Tom Nelson thinks young people are better parents.

_____ 9. Tom Nelson thinks smaller families are better.

_____ 10. Tom Nelson thinks young parents are stronger.

Discussion Activities

Directions: *Discuss these topics as a class or in a small group.*

1. Do you agree with Dr. Bernbaum or Tom Nelson? Why?

2. Based on your own experiences, how do American families differ from families in your country?

3. Describe the ideal marriage. Discuss the best age to get married, the number of children, where to live, and so forth.

4. Interview people who are not in your class. Ask them if they think people should be younger or older when they marry. What do most people think?

The Single Parent: One Woman's Story

Directions: *Read quickly. Your teacher will time you. Put your reading rate on Chart 1 in the back of this book.*

There are many single parents because there are many divorces in the United States. A young woman who gets married must think carefully about having a child. There is a 50 percent chance that she will have to take care of that child alone someday. Here is the story of one single parent who is happy with her life.   11 22 36 51 59

"My name is Sara. I am a secretary for a businessman in a small city. I have two daughters and a son. I was divorced three years ago. My ex-husband, Ron, comes to see the children one or two times a month. He usually takes them to a movie or a restaurant.   73 88 101 111

The life of a single parent is hard. I work all of the time. I work at my job all day. Then I go home to work all evening. I am often tired   128 144

Figure 38   A single parent and her children

when I get home at 5:30 in the evening. Tired or not, I make dinner for   160
my children and listen to their problems. After dinner, I clean the house,   173
wash clothes, shop for food, or help the children with their homework.   185
My children are young, but they help me around the house.   196

My biggest problem is money. When Ron and I divorced, he let me   208
have the small house the children and I live in. I'm glad I have it because 224
it's good for the children. Now I have to pay for it every month and pay   239
the bills. That's difficult. I make about $18,000 a year at my job. Ron has 254
to pay me $450 a month to help with the children. Everything is very   269
expensive now. There isn't enough money for everything. I have to be   281
very careful.   284

Do I want to marry again? Maybe. I'm going to be very careful. If I   299
marry again, I want to be sure it will be a good marriage this time. I   315
don't want to hurry. I am happier by myself than in a bad marriage."   329

READING SKILLS EXERCISES

Reading to Find Information

Directions: *Read the question. Then move your eyes over the paragraph that follows. It is not necessary to read every word carefully. Just look for the answer to the question. Put a line under the answer. Work quickly.*

How many children does Sara have?

My name is Sara. I am a secretary for a businessman in a small city. I have two daughters and a son. I was divorced three years ago. My ex-husband, Ron, comes to see the children one or two times a month. He usually takes them to a movie or a restaurant.

Reading to Find the Main Idea

Directions: *Read the three titles. Then read the paragraph. Choose the title that is best for the whole paragraph.*

a. The Life of a Single Parent Is Difficult
b. Children Should Help the Parent
c. Why Sara Is Tired

The life of a single parent is hard. I work all of the time. I work at my job all day. Then I go home to work all evening. I am often tired when I get home at 5:30 in the evening. Tired or not, I make dinner for my children and listen to their problems. After dinner, I clean the house, wash clothes, shop for food, or help the children with their homework. My children are young, but they help me around the house.

Using the Context

Directions: *You don't always need to know all of the words in a story. You can still understand the ideas. Read the following paragraph or paragraphs. Don't worry about the blanks at first. Answer the true/false questions for all paragraphs. Then go back and fill in the blanks, choosing a word from the following list.*

My biggest _____ is money. In the divorce, Ron let me have the
1

small house the children and I live in. I'm glad I have it because it's good for the

children. Now I have to pay the _____ every month and pay the bills.
2

That's difficult. I make a salary of $18,000 a year. Ron has to pay me $450 a

month for _____.
3

_____ Sara lives in an apartment and pays rent every month.

There are many single parents in the _____ because there are
1

many divorces. A young woman who gets married must _____
2

carefully about having a child. There is a 50 percent chance that she will have to

take care of that _____ alone someday.
3

_____ Fifty percent of the mothers in the United States take care of children

alone.

country	problem
child	child support
think	divorce
mortgage	marriage
	help

Timed Reading

Directions: *Read the timed reading again. Your teacher will time your reading. Put your reading rate on Chart 2 in the back of this book.*

Timed Reading Comprehension Check

Directions:
1. *Answer all the questions about the timed reading.*
2. *Go back to the timed reading and check your answers. Put a line under the answer in the timed reading. In the blank, write the line number where you found the answer in the timed reading.*
3. *When you have finished, your teacher may ask you to talk about the answers in a small group. In your group, try to agree on the answers, and then report back to the class.*

Line
Number   *Answer*

_____   _____   1. What work does Sara do in the evening?
   a. wash clothes
   b. go to the movies
   c. shop for food
   d. a and c

_____   _____   2. Does Sara want to marry again?
   a. yes
   b. no
   c. maybe

True/False:

_____   _____   3. Sara has $25,000 a year altogether.

_____   _____   4. A woman should not have a child if she can't take care of it alone.

_____   _____   5. Sara's biggest problem is that she is tired all of the time.

Directions: *Choose one word from the list to put in each blank.*

believe in   average
grown-up   interviewer
counselor

1. The _____ number of children in American families is two.

2. Sometimes it is difficult for divorced people to _____ marriage.

3. The _____ asks Sara questions about her children.

4. Sara and her husband didn't talk to a marriage _____.

5. _____ people can take care of the problems of marriage better.

chapter 11 _____

The Right to Die

Introduction

Directions: *Talk about these questions before you read the story.*

How do doctors know when a person is dead?

Has a good friend or someone in your family died in the last few years?

Should doctors try to save everybody?

Directions: *Read the story quickly. Try to guess the meaning of new words. Don't use your dictionary.*

What should we do with someone who is very sick or hurt and can't get better? This is a difficult problem, and it is not easy for anyone to decide. Imagine a problem such as this: Suppose your father has a car accident. He is hurt badly and is unconscious; that is, he can't think, speak, or hear. You take him to the hospital. The doctors tell you that his brain is dead, but they can help him breathe with a machine. The doctors tell you that your father will never wake up again.

Now you must answer some big questions. Do you think he is dead? Do you want the doctors to use the machine to make your father breathe?

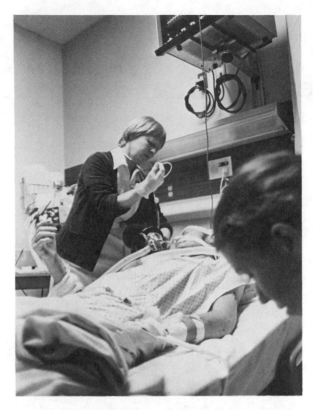

Figure 39 A person on life support machines

Sometimes machines can make an unconscious person breathe for years. If his brain is dead, however, he will never think, speak, or hear again. Do you want the doctors not to use the machine and let your father die?

Someone who is unconscious can't say he or she wants to die. Can his or her family make that decision? Some people think this is a good idea. Some think it is a bad idea. We will interview two people so we can hear both sides of this question. Read both opinions and then decide for yourself. What do you think?

First, we will talk to Doctor Benjamin Burns, who works in a big city hospital.

Interviewer: Dr. Burns, what should doctors do when a person's brain is hurt very badly?

Doctor Burns: When someone's brain is dead, doctors should let him die. When this person is unconscious, the family can decide for him.

Interviewer: What are your reasons?

Doctor Burns: Hospitals are very expensive. A family shouldn't spend all of its money to keep someone on machines. Doctors, hospitals, and machines should help the people who can get better. They shouldn't waste time on people who will never wake up again.

Interviewer: What about the family close to the dying person?

Doctor Burns: Many people are hurt when machines keep a person alive. If the unconscious person doesn't feel pain, the family and friends do. Machines only make the family and friends hurt longer. The sick person will finally die anyway.

Next, we will talk to Ms. Pam Roland. Her brother nearly died in a traffic accident nine years ago. The doctors thought that he was dead. Today he is alive and has a job and family.

Interviewer: What do you think about this problem? Can any person decide when someone should die?

Pam Roland: No person can decide when someone should die. Doctors should help a sick or hurt person. A doctor shouldn't let a person die.

Interviewer: Why do you say that?

Pam Roland: Someone may say a person can never get well again. Doctors can be wrong. Anything is possible. Anything can happen. Doctors might learn something to help this person in the future. If we let him die, we will never know.

Interviewer: Doctors have a difficult problem. What should they do in this situation?

Pam Roland: Hospitals and doctors have a job to do. Their job is to save lives and to fight death. A doctor who lets someone die is not doing his job.

Check Your Guess

Directions: *You guessed the meaning of these words from this story. Circle the letter beside the answer that gives the same idea as the new word. Do not use a dictionary.*

1. Imagine a problem such as this: Suppose your father has a car accident.
    a. tell
    b. hear
    c. think about

2. Suppose your father has a car <u>accident</u>. He is hurt badly and is <u>unconscious</u>; that is, he can't think, speak, or hear.

   a. wheel   a. asleep

   b. two cars park   b. can't think, speak, or hear

   c. two cars hit together   c. awake

3. The doctors tell you that his brain is dead. However, they can help him <u>breathe</u> with a machine.

   a. take in air

   b. see

   c. die

4. Hospitals are very <u>expensive</u>. A family shouldn't spend all of its money to keep someone on machines.

   a. cheap

   b. very bad

   c. cost a lot of money

Comprehension Exercises

Part 1: *You can find the answers to these questions in the story. You may look back to find an answer if you don't remember.*

1. Who are the two people interviewed in this reading?

2. Where does the doctor work?

3. Tell a reason for letting someone die.

4. Who nearly died in a traffic accident nine years ago?

5. Tell a reason for keeping sick or hurt people alive.

Part 2: *You may not find the answers to these questions in the story, but you can answer the questions if you understand the ideas.*

1. Can a machine help a person to live when the brain is dead?

2. When is a person unconscious?

3. When does Dr. Burns think we should let a person die?

4. What does Pam Roland think the job of a doctor is?

5. Look at Figure 40. What do you think Americans do with dead people? What happens to dead people in other countries?

Comprehension Check

Directions: *Read each sentence. Write T if it is true. Write F if it is false. Do not look back in the story.*

_____   1. Car accidents can hurt or kill people.

_____   2. We can read when we are unconscious.

_____   3. Machines can't help people stay alive if their brain is dead.

_____   4. Doctors and hospitals can help all people get better.

_____   5. Hospitals are cheap.

Figure 40   A cemetery is a place to bury dead people.

_____ 6. Dr. Burns thinks that doctors should let some people die.

_____ 7. Pam Roland thinks that doctors should let some people die.

_____ 8. Pam Roland thinks that doctors and hospitals in the future might know more about helping people.

_____ 9. Dr. Burns thinks that hospitals should only help people who can get better.

_____ 10. Pam Roland thinks the family should decide for a person who is unconscious.

Discussion Activities

Directions: *Discuss these topics as a class or in a small group.*

1. Do you agree with Dr. Burns or Pam Roland? Why?

2. Do you think there is an answer different from theirs?

3. Interview people who are not in your class. Ask them if they think unconscious people should be kept alive by machines. What do most people think?

4. According to different religions, what happens to a person after death?

5. Play the game of Scruples: Prepare enough 3 x 5 cards for each class member to have one. On one side of the card, write *yes, no,* or *it depends.* Shuffle the cards and deal one to each class member at random. Then the teacher writes a moral dilemma on the blackboard. Each student must respond to the dilemma according to the word on his or her card. If the card is a *yes* card, the student must take the affirmative side of the question, and so forth. Students can pair off to argue the question or, alternatively, the affirmatives can work in a group to prepare an answer, the negatives in a group, and those with *it depends* in a group. Following are some samples of moral dilemmas. The teacher should be able to prepare others that have some relevance to the class members.

   a. Your neighbor's six-year-old son asks you if there really is a Santa Claus. Should you tell him?

   b. You see someone in your class cheating on an exam. Should you tell your teacher?

   c. You find a wallet with $100 in it on the sidewalk in front of your school. Should you keep it?

   d. All countries should stop making nuclear weapons.

What Is It Like to Die?

Directions: *Read quickly. Your teacher will time you. Put your reading rate on Chart 1 in the back of this book.*

Doctors know more and more about how to save lives. They have	12
new machines and medicines to help them. Now they can save many	24
people who are dead or almost dead. During the past ten years, many	37
people died. Doctors brought some of them to life again. It is interesting	50
to ask them what it was like to die.	59
Dr. Raymond Moody is a doctor. He has heard many stories from	61
people who died or almost died. He has asked 150 of them what it was	76
like. They have told very interesting stories. He was surprised because	87
the stories were almost all the same. Here is one of the stories:	100
A woman is dying. Her body feels very bad. She hears the doctor	113
say that she is dead. Then she begins to hear a very loud noise in her	129
ears. She feels like she is moving or falling very quickly through a long,	143
dark place. After this, she thinks she is outside of her real body. She is	158
standing far away looking at her own body. People can't see her outside	171
of her body. From far away she watches the doctors and nurses try to	185
save her. She tries to get back into her real body, but she can't. She tries	201
to speak to the doctors, but they can't hear her.	211
Then she sees the faces of family and friends who died before her.	224
They are very happy. They come to help her. They tell her not to worry.	239
She begins to feel better.	244
Then a person in a bright light comes to the woman. The person in	258
the light asks the woman about her life. "Are you ready to die?" "What	272
did you do with your life?" These questions make the woman think. She	285
quickly remembers all of her life.	291
The woman comes to a door. She can go through it to death or back	306
to her body and life. Now she doesn't want to go back because she feels	321
happy. She feels love and peace with the person in the light. The doctors	335
do something to save her. She doesn't go through the door. Suddenly	347
she is back in her real body. She wakes up and she is alive. She doesn't	363
understand why.	365
Later, she tries to tell other people what happened. It is difficult to	378
find the words to tell the story. Other people don't understand, so she	391
doesn't tell it anymore. She thinks it is the most important thing that	404

ever happened to her. It changes her life. She knows it wasn't a dream.   418
For the rest of her life she tries to learn many things and to love other   434
people. She is not afraid of death now. She knows that many things go   448
on after death but in a different way.   456

There are many stories from all over the world, from different   467
people and different times. Many of the stories are the same. Maybe the   480
stories are true. What do you think? If we know about death, will we   494
change the way we live?   499

READING SKILLS EXERCISES

Reading to Find Information

Directions: *Read the question. Then move your eyes over the paragraph that follows it. It is not necessary to read every word carefully. Just look for the answer to the question. Put a line under the answer. Work quickly.*

What is the second thing the dying woman hears?

A woman is dying. Her body feels very bad. She hears the doctor say that she is dead. Then she begins to hear a very loud noise in her ears. She feels like she is moving or falling very quickly through a long, dark place. After this, she thinks she is outside of her real body. She is standing far away, looking at her own body. People can't see her outside of her body. From far away she watches the doctors and nurses try to save her. She tries to get back into her real body, but she can't. She tries to speak to the doctors, but they can't hear her. She feels very much alone.

Reading to Find the Main Idea

Directions: *Read the three titles. Then read the paragraph. Choose the title that is best for the whole paragraph.*

a. It Is Interesting to Almost Die
b. Doctors Know More about How to Save Lives
c. People Who Died Can Tell Us about Death

Doctors know more and more about how to save lives. They have new machines and medicines to help them. Now they can save many people who are dead or who almost died. During the past ten years, many people died. Doctors brought some of them to life again. It is interesting to ask them what it was like to die.

Using the Context

Directions: *You don't always need to know all of the words in a story. You can still understand the ideas. Read the following paragraph or paragraphs. Don't worry about the blanks at first. Answer the true/false questions for all paragraphs. Then go back and fill in the blanks, choosing a word from the following list.*

The woman _____ the door. She can pass through it to death or
1
_____ to her body and life. Now she doesn't want to go back because
2
she feels happy. She feels love and peace with the person in the light. The
doctors do something to save her. She doesn't _____ through the
3
door. Suddenly, she is back in her _____ body. She wakes up and she
4
is alive. She doesn't understand why.

_____ She doesn't pass through the door because the doctors do
something to save her.

Later she tries to tell other _____ what happened. It is difficult to
1
find the words to tell the story. Other people don't understand, so she doesn't
tell it anymore. She thinks it is the most _____ thing that ever
2
happened to her. It changes her _____. She knows it wasn't a dream.
3
For the rest of her life she tries to learn many things and to love other people.
She is not _____ of death now. She knows that _____ things
4   5
go on after death but in a different way.

_____ People understand her story.

important	afraid	approaches	peace
many	natural	pass	ready
people	return	difficult	dying
life			

Timed Reading

Directions: *Read the timed reading again. Your teacher will time your reading. Put your reading rate on Chart 2 in the back of this book.*

Timed Reading Comprehension Check

Directions: 1. *Answer all the questions about the timed reading.*

2. *Go back to the timed reading and check your answers. Put a line under the answer in the timed reading. In the blank, write the line number where you found the answer in the timed reading.*

3. *When you have finished, your teacher may ask you to talk about the answers in a small group. In your group, try to agree on the answers, and then report back to the class.*

*Line
Number   Answer*

_____   _____   1. Many of the stories about death around the world are
a. alike.
b. different.
c. false.

_____   _____   2. The person in the bright light
a. asks the woman if she wants to die.
b. asks her about the door.
c. asks her if she is ready to die.

_____   _____   3. Which of the following sentences is true?
a. What happened to the dying woman makes her afraid of death.
b. What happened to the dying woman makes her not afraid of death.
c. What happened to the dying woman makes her interested in death.

_____   _____   4. Implied but not stated in this story (that is, the idea is in the story but not in the same words):
a. Death is easy for all people.
b. We shouldn't be afraid of death.
c. We should worry about death.

True/False:

_____   _____   5. Dead family and friends will help you when you die.

Directions: *Choose one word from the list to put in each blank.*

expensive	unconscious
breathe	imagine

1. _____ what it is like to die.

2. A man is _____. He needs a machine to help him _____.

3. Hospitals and machines are _____.

What Will Atomic War Be Like?

Directions: *Your teacher may use this as a timed reading in class or let you read it by yourself outside of class.*

What will happen if there is an atomic war? The whole war may	13
take about 30 to 60 minutes from beginning to end. Fifty thousand	25
atomic bombs are ready to go to most cities in the United States, Russia,	39
Europe, and China.	42

Every city with 25,000 people or more in those countries will get a	55
bomb. Where a bomb hits, nothing will be left for many miles around.	68
All of the people there will be killed. There will be many large fires from	83
the bombs. Fires will burn most of the plants and animals. Fires will melt	97
the ice at the North and South Poles.	105

Radiation from the bombs will fall on the earth. Radiation is the	117
part of the bomb left after the bomb explodes. The wind will blow it	131
around the world. It will get into the food, air, and water. Some people	145
may not die from the bombs. They will die later from the radiation.	158
Radiation will kill people after they eat food or drink water with	170
radiation in it.	173

There will be many more diseases after the war. They will kill many	186
people. If any people are still alive after that, they may get cancer very	200
easily. Any children people have after the war may not be normal and	213
healthy. People who are not killed in the war will not live long after it.	228
Everyone will die if there is an atomic war. No one will win an atomic	243
war.	244

Comprehension Check

Directions: *Choose the correct answer. Write the letter in the blank.*

_____ 1. An atomic war will
  a. destroy the earth.
  b. kill many people.
  c. melt the ice at the North and South Poles.
  d. all of the above.

_____ 2. People in an atomic war will die from
  a. fire.
  b. radiation.
  c. the falling bombs.
  d. all of the above.

     3. It is probably false that an atomic war·will
       a. destroy many things.
       b. last a very long time.
       c. start with Russia and the United States.

     4. It is true that
       a. no one will win in an atomic war.
       b. the United States will win an atomic war.
       c. everyone will win in an atomic war.

True/False:

     5. If you have been near radiation, you can get cancer easier.

     6. Radiation doesn't hurt unborn babies.

     7. If you live in a small town, you may not have to worry about atomic war.

     8. After an atomic war, there will be a problem with what people eat and drink.

     9. Some people will live after an atomic war.

    10. Atomic war may kill all people and animals.

chapter 12 _____

Memory

Introduction

Directions: *Talk about these questions before you read the story.*

What things are easy for you to remember? What are difficult?

What can you do if you forget something important?

Do you use any special ways to help you remember?

Directions: *Read the story quickly. Try to guess the meaning of new words. Don't use your dictionary.*

We know an address, such as 193 Main Street, a telephone number, such as 431–7689, and how to tie our shoes. We keep all three of these pieces of information in our brain in our memory. We can use them when we need them.

There are three parts to memory:

1. Sensory information
2. Short-term memory
3. Long-term memory

Sensory information goes into the memory. These are things we see, hear, taste, smell, or touch (our five senses). If something happens and we have strong feelings along with it or we use more than one of our senses, it is easier to remember. For example, it is easier to remember the details of our car accident than a friend's telephone number. In the car accident we see, hear, feel; we are afraid, and we use many senses.

The next step in memory is short-term memory. Short-term memory makes it possible for us to remember a question long enough to answer it. Then we forget the question when we are finished. We can usually remember only about nine numbers at the same time in our short-term memory. So short-term memory helps us remember a telephone number long enough to call; then we forget it.

We choose some information to go into our long-term memory if we think we may need it more than a few minutes in the future. We can remember a special birthday when we were six years old, but probably we don't remember every birthday we have had. Information goes into our long-term memory either (a) because it was very exciting or important or (b) because we practiced it. If we repeat a name or our telephone number over and over again, it will go into our long-term memory. We memorize it.

People remember better if they think about pictures when they try to put information into long-term memory. For example, in one study scientists put students into two groups. Group 1 studied 12 lists of vocabulary words. There were 10 words on each list. The scientists told them to learn the words any way they could. Group 2 was given the same word lists to study. But these students organized the words into lists so that each list was about one idea. Then they made up an exciting story using the words on each list. They pictured the story in their minds. When they took a test, the first group remembered 14 percent of the words. Group 2 remembered 93 percent of the words.

Check Your Guess

Directions: *You guessed the meaning of these words from this story. Circle the letter beside the answer that gives the same idea as the new word.*

1. These are things we see, hear, taste, smell, or touch.
   a. our five senses
   b. something that we know
   c. pictures

2. Information goes into our long-term memory because it was very <u>exciting</u> or important.
   a. makes strong feeling
   b. correct
   c. necessary

3. Information goes into our long-term memory because we <u>practiced</u> it. If we repeat a telephone number over and over again, it will go into our long-term memory.

    a. tried it

    b. read it

    c. did it over and over

4. It is easier to remember the <u>details</u> of a car accident than our friend's telephone number.

    a. the main idea

    b. the small parts

    c. the whole picture

5. It goes into our long-term memory. We <u>memorize</u> it.

    a. forget it

    b. say it

    c. remember

6. These students <u>organized</u> the words into lists so that each list was about one idea.

    a. put in order

    b. memorized

    c. moved

Comprehension Exercises

Part 1: *You can find the answers to these questions in the story. You may look back to find an answer if you don't remember.*

1. What are our five senses?

2. What goes into the memory?

3. How many numbers can we usually remember at the same time?

4. Which group remembered more vocabulary words?

Part 2: *You may not find the answers to these questions in the story. You can answer the questions if you understand the ideas in the story.*

1. How can you put information into your long-term memory?

2. What can you use your short-term memory for?

3. What is a good way to learn vocabulary words?

Comprehension Check

Directions: *Read each sentence. Write T if it is true. Write F if it is false. Do not look back in the story.*

_____ 1. It is easier to remember grammar rules than your boyfriend's or girlfriend's telephone number.

_____ 2. You hear the telephone ring. This is sensory information.

_____ 3. You probably remember every birthday you have had.

_____ 4. One way to remember something is to practice it.

_____ 5. You can remember 12 numbers at the same time.

_____ 6. You remember how to tie your shoes with your short-term memory.

_____ 7. Thinking about pictures can help you remember.

_____ 8. It is easier to learn information if it is organized.

_____ 9. If you repeat something over and over, it will go into your short-term memory.

_____ 10. With our five senses we can taste, see, hear, smell, and touch.

Discussion Activities

Directions: *Discuss these topics as a class or in a small group.*

1. Play the memory game. On 3 x 5 cards, make two sets of cards numbered 1 through 10. Shuffle the cards and deal them face down in rows of five each. Turn over any two cards and try to make a match. If you don't make a match, turn the cards face down again. Another person can turn over any two cards and try to make a match. Try to remember where the numbers are. If you make a match, you take the two cards and play again. You can continue to turn

over cards as long as you make a match. The person with the most cards when all of the cards are finished wins the game. The teacher can experiment with putting different material on the cards—for example, pictures, vocabulary words, or material relating to your other classes.

2. Organization exercise.

It is easier to memorize a large group of words if you organize them so that they are in groups that mean something. For example, look at this list of words:

village	pencil
paper	city
state	student
teacher	town
country	book

It is easier to memorize the words in shorter lists and in lists that mean something:

teacher	village
student	town
book	city
paper	state
pencil	country

Another way to memorize better is to make a story from the words. For example:

teacher	The teacher gave the student a book, but he didn't have a
student	pencil or paper.
book	A small group of houses make a village. Larger than a village is
pencil	a town. Larger than a town is a city. Larger than a city is a state.
paper	Larger than a state is a country.
village	

As a class activity, organize the following words into four lists of five words each. Then divide the class into two teams. Each team should make up a funny or exciting story using two lists of words. Think of the pictures that go with the story. Tomorrow your teacher will test you to see how many words on your list you can remember. The team that remembers the most words wins the game.

walked	hat
Mr. Smith	meat
son	dropped
eggs	dog
coat	fell
daughter	bread
wife	keys
milk	gloves
apple	ate
car	lost

Studying to Remember

Directions: *Read quickly. Your teacher will time you. Put your reading rate on Chart 1 in the back of this book.*

Students want to find the best way to put information into their 12
long-term memories. They want to be able to remember the information 23
later when they take a test. What is the best way to learn information so 38
that they can remember it when they want to? 47

When you study, you should read the whole lesson first. This gives 59
you the whole picture in which to put the ideas. New information that 72
fits into the whole picture is easier to remember than separate facts. You 85
also learn faster if you look at headings, introductions, important words, 96
summaries, conclusions, and anything else that helps to organize the 106
material. Organized material is easier to understand. 113

After you read a whole lesson, the next step is to study the parts. 127
Think about how they fit into the whole picture. 136

Figure 41   In the Perry-Castenada Library, University of Texas at Austin

If you have a lot to study, don't try to do the whole job at once.   152
Learning should be spread out and spaced. This gives the information   163
time to "sink in." You should study grammar three times, a half hour   176
each time. That is better than studying for an hour and a half all at one   192
time. Even shorter study periods are better for vocabulary lists and other   204
difficult material. To learn the most in a two-hour study session, study   216
different kinds of material: a half hour on grammar, 15 minutes on   228
vocabulary, 20 minutes on writing, and so on. The change will help to   241
keep you interested.   244

You forget most quickly right after you read or hear something   255
new. You should review right away so you won't forget, and if possible,   268
explain it to someone else. When you review and test yourself on the   281
material, you are being active; active learning is better than just reading   293
or listening. You remember more and save time in the end if you spend   307
at least one-third of your time on active review.   316

READING SKILLS EXERCISES

Reading to Find Information

Directions: *Read the question. Then move your eyes over the paragraph that follows it. It is not necessary to read every word carefully. Just look for the answer to the question. Put a line under the answer. Work quickly.*

How much time should you spend on active review?

You forget most quickly right after you read or hear something new. You should review right away so you won't forget, and if possible, explain it to someone else. When you review and test yourself on the material, you are being active; active learning is better than just reading or listening. You remember more and save time in the end if you spend at least one-third of your time on active review.

Reading to Find the Main Idea

Directions: *Read the three titles. Then read the paragraph. Choose the title that is best for the whole paragraph.*

a. Steps for Good Studying
b. How to Organize Material
c. The Importance of the Whole Picture

When you study, you should read the whole lesson first. This gives you the whole picture in which to put the ideas. New information that fits into the whole picture is easier to remember than separate facts. You also learn faster if you look at headings, introductions, important words, summaries, conclusions and anything else that helps to organize the material. Organized material is easier to understand.

Using the Context

Directions: *You don't always need to know all of the words in a story. You can still understand the ideas. Read the following paragraph or paragraphs. Don't worry about the blanks at first. Answer the true/false question. Then go back and fill in the blanks, choosing a word from the following list.*

If you have a lot to study, don't try to do the whole job at once. Learning should be spread out and spaced. This gives the information time to "sink in." You should study grammar three times, a half hour each time. That is better than studying for an hour and a half all at one time. Even _____ study

₁

periods are better for vocabulary lists and other _____ material. To

₂

learn the most in a two-hour study time, study different kinds of material: a half hour on grammar, 15 minutes on _____, 20 minutes on writing and so

₃

on. The _____ will help to keep you interested.

₄

_____ Vocabulary lists are more difficult to learn than grammar.

change	forget
difficult	spread out
vocabulary	active
shorter	

Timed Reading

Directions: *Read the timed reading again. Your teacher will time your reading. Put your reading rate on Chart 2 in the back of this book.*

Timed Reading Comprehension Check

Directions: *1. Answer all the questions about the timed reading.*

2. Go back to the timed reading and check your answers. Put a line under the answer in the timed reading. In the blank, write the line number where you found the answer in the timed reading.

3. When you have finished, your teacher may ask you to talk about the answers in a small group. In your group try to agree on the answers, and then report back to the class.

Line Number	Answer	True/False:
_____	_____	1. To review, reading the lesson again is better than testing yourself.
_____	_____	2. Being interested in the information is not necessarily important.
_____	_____	3. Many short study periods are better than one long one.
_____	_____	4. The night before a test is the best time to review.
_____	_____	5. Organized material is easier to understand.

Directions: *Choose one word from the list to put in each blank.*

exciting	memorize
detail	information
practice	organized

1. Students want to know the best way to put _____ into their long-term memories.

2. _____ material is easier to understand.

3. The movie was so _____, I can remember every little _____.

4. I play the piano. In order to _____ a piece of music, I have to _____ every day.

SUPPLEMENTAL READING

Hypnotism

Directions: *Your teacher may use this as a timed reading in class or let you read it by yourself outside of class.*

Hypnotism is very old. Thousands of years ago, people started to use it in Egypt. The use of hypnotism has expanded greatly since that time. Today, doctors and scientists in almost every country hypnotize people to help them with their problems.

What is hypnotism, and how does it work? Many people think that a hypnotist puts people to sleep. Then he makes the hypnotized people do strange things. This is not what a hypnotist does. Hypnotism is really just a way to relax the mind and body.

What are some of the uses of hypnotism? We go to a hypnotist because we have a problem. The problem makes us unhappy. The hypnotist asks us to think hard about something and relax. When we are relaxed, the hypnotist gives us some ideas to help us with our problems.

A baseball player says that hypnotism helped him. He went to a hypnotist because he had a problem when he hit the ball. Once a ball hit him in the face. After that he was afraid that the ball might hit him again. He didn't hit the ball well after that. The hypnotist told the player to relax. Then he told him to think about the many times he had hit the ball well. After that, the baseball player was not afraid. He hit the ball better.

Hypnotism can help people to remember things. The police sometimes ask hypnotists to help them. For example, a man sees an accident. He forgets the license number of the car he sees. If he is hypnotized, he may remember it. The police can then find the car and catch the driver.

People who are hypnotized can also make mistakes or say something that isn't true. People remember what they think they saw. That may not be what really happened.

The police don't hypnotize people who do something wrong. People who are hypnotized may say something that isn't true. A person who has done something bad has a good reason to say something that isn't true.

Comprehension Check

Directions: *Read each sentence. Write T if it is true. Write F if it is false. Do not look back in the story.*

_____ 1. Hypnotists don't put people to sleep.

_____ 2. People use hypnotism because they have a problem.

_____ 3. Hypnotism makes us do strange things.

_____ 4. People use hypnotism a lot now.

_____ 5. The baseball player was afraid to play baseball.

_____ 6. The police always ask hypnotists to help them.

_____ 7. Hypnotism can always help you remember things.

_____ 8. People who are hypnotized can say something that isn't true.

_____ 9. Hypnotized people can make mistakes.

_____ 10. The police often hypnotize people who do something wrong.

Word Families Vocabulary Exercise

Directions: _Words have different forms depending on how they are used in a sentence, but the meaning of the word usually doesn't change. You can increase your vocabulary by recognizing the different forms of a word._

Noun	Verb	Adjective	Adverb
division	divide	divisible	
solution	solve	solvable	
prediction	predict	predictable	predictably
excitement	excite	excited	excitedly
		exciting	
organization	organize	organized	
value	value	valuable	valuably
belief	believe	believable	believably
action	act	active	actively
memory	memorize	memorable	memorably
	remember		
movement	move	moving	movingly

Directions: _Choose the correct form of one of the preceding words to fill in the blanks._

1. The weather forecaster makes a _____ about the weather for the next day.

2. Scientists cannot _____ all the problems of life.

3. What is the _____ of the dollar around the world today?

4. We were very _____ by the football game.

5. The old man said that his _____ was not as good as it used to be.

chapter 13 _____

The Brain

Introduction

Directions: *Talk about these questions before you read the story.*

What do you know about the brain?

How does it work?

What does it do?

How are the brains of humans different from animals?

Directions: *Read the story quickly. Try to guess the meaning of new words. Don't use your dictionary.*

The brain tells the other parts of the body what to do. We think with our brain. We understand the world around us with our brain. However, doctors do not know much about how the brain works. Doctors can do many things with other parts of the body. They can give a person a new heart. They can put an arm back on after it has been cut off.

It is easy to study some parts of the body, but it is difficult to know how the brain works. It is difficult to work on a brain. If the brain is without enough blood for three to five minutes, the brain dies. So when doctors work on the brain, they have only three to five minutes to do their work. Doctors try new things on the brain, but they must be very careful. The brain is the center of those things that make us what we are.

What are some of the things doctors know about the brain? The brain has three parts: the medulla, the cerebellum, and the cerebrum. The medulla is at the top of the spinal cord. It is inside the skull at the bottom part of the brain. The medulla is the busiest part of the brain. All information that the brain gets must come through the medulla. All answers must go through the medulla on their way back to the body. A hit to the back of the neck can kill a person if it hurts the medulla.

The cerebellum is above and behind the medulla. It is about the size of a small ball. People can walk, dance, and play games because of the cerebellum. Some doctors say the medulla and cerebellum are parts of an older brain. This brain was in animals before there were human beings. We feel hungry because our old, or lower, brain is working. We breathe and our hearts work because of this part of the brain. Sometimes scientists call the old brain the feeling brain.

The cerebrum is the thinking brain, or the higher brain. It is the biggest part. It is above the medulla and cerebellum. The cerebrum takes up most of the space in the head. It is the part of the brain that makes us intelligent human beings.

The cerebrum folds over on itself because it is large and in a small space. It is like a big piece of paper that we make into a small ball. The name of these folds is convolutions. The human brain has many convolutions. Other animals do not have many, so lower animals do not have much brain. The convolutions are very important because they let us get more information from the world.

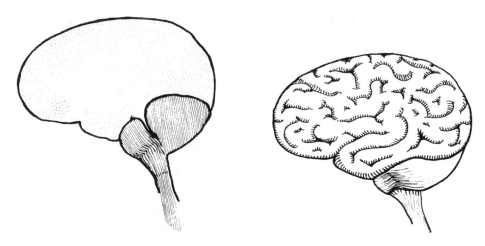

Figure 42   The brain

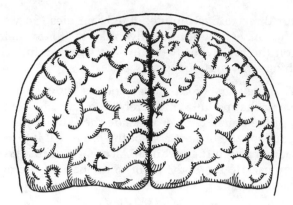

Figure 43   The cerebrum

The cerebrum is not just one piece. It has two parts, or hemispheres, the left and the right. Each hemisphere takes care of one side of the body. The left hemisphere of the brain gets information from the right side of the body. It takes care of the right side of the body. The right hemisphere takes care of the left side of the body. We can think, remember, see, speak, write, and decide because of the cerebral hemispheres.

Check Your Guess

Directions: *You guessed the meaning of these words from this story. Circle the letter beside the answer that gives the same idea as the new word. Do not use a dictionary.*

1. Doctors try new things on the brain, but they must be very careful. The brain is <u>the center</u> of those things that make us what we are.

   a. the most important part

   b. the biggest part

   c. the side

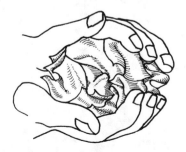

Figure 44   An example of folds

2. The cerebrum <u>folds</u> over on itself because it is large and in a small space. It is like a big piece of paper that we make into a ball.

    a. one part lies on another part

    b. one part cuts another part

    c. one part sees another part

3. The cerebrum folds over on itself because it is large and in a small space. It is like a big piece of paper that we make into a ball. The name of these folds is <u>convolutions</u>.

    a. parts

    b. papers

    c. folds

4. The <u>cerebrum</u> is the thinking brain, or the higher brain. It is the biggest part. It is above the medulla and cerebellum. It is the part of the brain that makes us intelligent human beings.

    a. the feeling part of the brain

    b. the intellectual part of the brain

    c. the part of the brain that gets and sends information

5. The <u>cerebellum</u> was part of an older brain. This brain was in animals before there were human beings.

    a. the feeling part of the brian

    b. the intellectual part of the brain

    c. the part of the brain that gets and sends information

6. The <u>medulla</u> is the busiest part of the brain. All information that the brain gets must come through the medulla. All answers must go through the medulla on their way back to the body.

    a. the feeling part of the brain

    b. the thinking part of the brain

    c. the part of the brain that gets and sends information

Comprehension Exercises

Part 1: *You can find the answers to these questions in the story. You may look back to find an answer if you don't remember.*

1. How long can the brain live without blood before it dies?

2. What are the three parts of the brain?

3. What is the busiest part of the brain?

4. What is the thinking part of the brain?

5. Who has the most convolutions of the brain, human beings or other animals?

Part 2: *You may not find the answers to these questions in the story. You can answer the questions if you understand the ideas in the story.*

1. Why can't doctors give a person a new brain?

2. Where does the brain get its information?

3. Do animals have a medulla?

4. Can we think without the cerebrum?

5. What part of the brain works first?

Comprehension Check

Directions: *Read each sentence. Write T if it is true. Write F if it is false. Do not look back in the story.*

_____ 1. Doctors can give a person a new heart.

_____ 2. The brain dies if it is without blood for 7 to 10 minutes.

_____ 3. The cerebellum is the busiest part of the brain.

_____ 4. Animals do not have brains.

_____ 5. The brain is smooth and flat.

_____ 6. The cerebrum has three parts.

_____ 7. The cerebrum is the feeling part of the brain.

_____ 8. Most animals have small cerebrums.

_____ 9. The right side of the brain takes care of the right arm.

_____ 10. The left side of the body takes care of the right side of the brain.

Discussion Activities

Directions: _Discuss these topics as a class or in a small group._

1. Do we use all of our brain?

2. What does our brain do when we sleep?

3. Can we live without our brain?

4. When do we say a person probably dies?

5. Find out if you have a dominant left brain or a dominant right brain. Here is a simple test developed by Jerre Levy. Write a few words on a paper, using your normal writing hand, and watch your hand as it moves. Is the pencil point toward you or away from you? Is your hand below the line of writing or is it curled up above it? People use two main styles of writing: straight or hooked. If you are a straight writer, you hold your hand below the line and your pencil points away from you. If you are a hooked writer, you curl your hand up over the line and hold the pencil pointing toward you.

   Straight right-handers have a dominant left brain.
   Hooked left-handers also have a dominant left brain.
   Straight left-handers have a dominant right brain.
   Hooked right-handers also have a dominant right brain.

   So only people (both right-handers and left-handers) who use the straight writing style have the normal criss-cross dominance.

6. After you read the timed reading, think about whether you use the left hemisphere or right hemisphere of your cerebrum more often. Most of us prefer one over the other, or we are more comfortable with one. Do you like to think in a more orderly way, step-by-step? Are you good at mathematics? Do you remember names and telephone numbers? You probably prefer your left hemisphere. Do you feel many feelings? Are you intuitive? Are you artistic or musical? Are you so poor in mathematics that you can't balance your checkbook? You probably prefer your right hemisphere.

   It is a good idea to practice using the other hemisphere so that both sides can be equally strong. Following are some activities to practice using your less developed hemisphere. Choose one activity, which you don't usually do, to practice. Talk to the class for one minute about the activity. Was it difficult? How did you feel? What did you learn?

Left Hemisphere Activities	Right Hemisphere Activities
1. Find out how a machine works	1. Go for a walk in the mountains, on the beach, or in a park. Feel that you are a part of nature.
2. Learn to use a personal computer.	2. Play with clay.
3. Go to see a movie; then write about what was good and bad in the movie.	3. Drive around, not going anyplace.
4. Put something together using instructions.	4. Go dancing.
5. Organize your records or books into groups.	5. Play with children the way they want to play.
6. Find a mistake in your bank account.	6. Take a break three times a day to see what you are feeling.
7. Organize your closet.	7. Make up something new to eat and eat it.
8. Be exactly on time all day.	8. Stay in bed 15 minutes in the morning when you wake up. Let your mind run freely and see what comes into your mind.

TIMED READING

Right Brain/Left Brain

Directions: *Read quickly. Your teacher will time you. Put your reading rate on Chart 1 in the back of this book.*

For a long time, most people thought the two hemispheres of the | 12
cerebrum were the same. Scientists have been studying the brain. Now | 23
they know that this is not true. One side of the cerebrum thinks in a | 38
different way from the other. | 43

Each hemisphere controls the movement and sense of touch of the | 54
opposite side of the body. The left hemisphere picks up and sends out | 67
most of the messages to and from the right side of the body. The right | 82
half of the cerebrum receives messages about what we feel from the left | 95
side of our body and sends messages to tell muscles on the left side to | 110
move. If you write with your right hand, your left hemisphere helps | 122
move your fingers. If you are left-handed, your right hemisphere moves | 133
your fingers. | 135

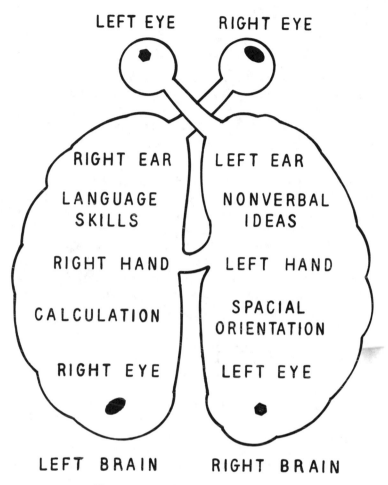

Figure 45 Left brain/right brain

In addition to taking care of the opposite side of the body, each hemisphere does its special part in thinking. The left hemisphere of the cerebrum is stronger for most of us in language ability. This is because it appears to work in a step-by-step way, keeping and sorting messages into an order that makes sense. The left hemisphere learns and remembers telephone numbers and people's names and does difficult mathematical problems. The right side of your brain understands such things as shape, size or pattern, music, art, and humor. It can solve problems, too, but not the way the left brain does. Instead of taking problems step-by-step, the right brain sees the whole picture and understands by insight and intuition.

148
160
174
185
196
205
215
228
241
251
256

Ninety-five percent of right-handed people have their language area in the left hemisphere. Sixty percent of left-handed people do too.

264
276

Only a few left-handers have their language area in the right   287
hemisphere. Some left-handers have their language centers divided   295
between the left and right hemispheres.   301

The two hemispheres of the cerebrum work together in all our   312
activities, each half using its own special skills and doing what it does 325
best. When you read a story, for example, your left hemisphere works 337
on the words to understand the meaning of the sentences. At the same 350
time, the right hemisphere understands the feelings that come from the 361
story.   362

Here is another example. You go to the grocery store to buy four   375
things. Your left hemisphere will help you remember those four things 386
all the way to the store. Your right hemisphere will help you remember 399
the way to the grocery store. When you went to the store before, you 413
didn't notice the name of the street, but you have a general idea of how 428
things look. Is the store on the right or left, is the building tall or short, 444
does the store have large windows in front? Your right hemisphere will 456
help you find the store by the way it looks and its location.   469

READING SKILLS EXERCISES

Reading to Find Information

Directions: *Read the question. Then move your eyes over the paragraph that follows it. It is not necessary to read every word carefully. Just look for the answer to the question. Put a line under the answer. Work quickly.*

How many right-handed people have their language area in the left hemisphere?

Ninety-five percent of right-handed people have their language area in the left hemisphere. Sixty percent of the left-handed people do too. Only a few left-handers have their language area in the right hemisphere. Some left-handers have their language centers divided between the left and right hemispheres.

Reading to Find the Main Idea

Directions: *Read the three titles. Then read the paragraph. Choose the title that is best for the whole paragraph.*

a. The Left Hemisphere Understands Meanings
b. The Right Hemisphere Understands Feelings
c. How the Two Hemispheres Work Together

The two hemispheres of the cerebrum work together in all our activities, each half using its own special skills and doing what it does best. When you read a story, for example, your left hemisphere works on the words to understand the meaning of the sentences. At the same time, the right hemisphere understands the feelings that come from the story.

Using the Context

Directions: *You don't always need to know all of the words in a story. You can still understand the ideas. Read the following paragraph or paragraphs. Don't worry about the blanks at first. Answer the true/false questions for all paragraphs. Then go back and fill in the blanks with a word you know.*

In addition to taking care of the _____ side of the body, each
                                        1
hemisphere does its special part in thinking. The left hemisphere of the

cerebrum is stronger for most of us in language ability. This is because it appears

to work in a step-by-step way, keeping and _____ messages into an
                                                   2
order that makes sense. The left hemisphere learns and remembers telephone

numbers and people's _____ and does difficult mathematical
                              3
problems. The right side of your brain understands such things as shape, size or

pattern, _____, art, and humor. It can solve problems too, but not the
                 4
way the left brain does. Instead of taking problems step-by-step, the right brain

_____ the whole picture and understands by insight and intuition.
        5

_____Only the left hemisphere can solve problems.

Timed Reading

Directions: *Read the timed reading again. Your teacher will time your reading. Put your reading rate on Chart 2 in the back of this book.*

Timed Reading Comprehension Check

Directions: 1. *Answer all the questions about the timed reading.*
2. *Go back to the timed reading and check your answers. Put a line under the answer in the timed reading. In the blank, write the line number where you found the answer in the timed reading.*

3. When you have finished, your teacher may ask you to talk about the answers in a small group. In your group, try to agree on the answers, and then report back to the class.

Line Number	Answer	True/False:
_____	_____	1. The two hemispheres think in the same way.
_____	_____	2. For most of us, language ability is located in the right hemisphere.
_____	_____	3. Artists have probably developed their right hemisphere.
_____	_____	4. If you have difficulty with mathematics, your left hemisphere is probably stronger.
_____	_____	5. If something happens to one hemisphere, you will have difficulty moving the opposite side of your body.

Directions: *Choose one word from the list to put in each blank.*

fold   message
location   cerebrum
                          convolutions

1. The human brain has more _____ than animals' brains.

2. Because the two hemispheres of the _____ work together, we can think, remember, see, speak, write, and decide.

3. After I wrote the letter, I had to _____ it to put it in the envelope.

4. I don't know where the grocery store is. I will ask a policeman for the

   _____.

5. My mother called while I was out. She left a _____ with my roommate.

Leonardo da Vinci

Directions: *Your teacher may use this as a timed reading in class or let you read it by yourself outside of class.*

Leonardo da Vinci was one of the most famous artists who ever lived. Thousands of people go to see his paintings *The Last Supper* and *The Creation* every year. His *Mona Lisa* in the Louvre Museum in Paris may be the most famous painting in the world.

Leonardo was born in 1452 in Vinci, a small town near Florence, Italy. When he was 14, his father sent him to study art with one of the best painters in Florence. Leonardo studied with him for about six years. Soon he became a better painter than his teacher.

When Leonardo went to live in Milan, he didn't need a job. Some people there believed in his artistic ability. They gave him money to live on; they were his *patrons*. He could use all his time to study and paint. He didn't need to worry about making money to pay for food and lodging. His patrons paid for everything.

Leonardo was more than a painter. He lived 500 years ago, but he had many ideas like scientists of today. He wanted to know everything. He studied many sciences. He studied about the human body and how the eye works. He also studied mathematics, the stars, the earth, plants, animals, and machines. He was interested in how things work.

After he studied the sciences, he began to draw plans for new machines. He drew plans for many kinds of machines that move by themselves. He drew plans for something for people to wear on their feet to walk on water. He didn't like war, but he drew plans for better machines for war.

For the last 25 years of his life, he wanted to fly like a bird. He studied birds to see how their wings worked. He drew plans to make wings for men so men could fly. He drew plans for a parachute, a helicopter, and other machines to help people fly.

We have thousands of his drawings to show us his idea of the future. He didn't get to see his ideas happen. Only in the last 100 years have people made machines like the ones that Leonardo drew. We now have parachutes and helicopters.

Leonardo was a genius, but his genius was in many different areas. This is unusual. He seemed to use the left and right sides of his brain equally well. He developed both hemispheres; he developed a *whole brain* view of life. Maybe this is the reason he was such a man of the future. He was ahead of his time.

Comprehension Questions

Directions: *Choose the correct answer. Put the correct letter in the blank.*

_____ 1. Leonardo studied
   a. mathematics.
   b. human and animal anatomy.
   c. the earth.
   d. plants.
   e. all of the above.

True/False:

_____ 2. In 1466, Leonardo went to Milan to study art.

_____ 3. Leonardo was only a painter.

_____ 4. The *Mona Lisa* is a painting by Michaelangelo.

_____ 5. Leonardo lived 600 years ago.

_____ 6. Vinci is a small town in Italy.

_____ 7. Leonardo liked war.

_____ 8. During the last 25 years of life, Leonardo wanted to fly.

_____ 9. A helicopter moves on the ground like a car.

_____ 10. Today there are machines like those in Leonardo's drawings.

chapter 14 _____

Computers

Introduction

Directions: *Talk about these questions before you read the story.*

What can computers do?

Name as many different uses for computers as you can.

Directions: *Read the story quickly. Try to guess the meaning of new words. Don't use your dictionary.*

The computer has changed our lives more than any other machine in the twentieth century.

Computers are fast. A new supercomputer can do over 250 million separate actions in one second. It can solve almost any problem if the problem can be broken down into small steps. Computers can take in very large amounts of information. They can organize it in any way. They can pull out a single fact in an instant and never forget. And computers are faster, better, smaller and cheaper all the time.

Computers are very important to our lives. In fact, it is hard to believe that we have only had them since 1946.

Figure 46   Supercomputer at National Center for Atmospheric Research

When a computer is used correctly and when it is in good repair, it never makes a mistake. Unfortunately, people run computers, and people make mistakes. The computer itself is a machine, and machines can break down.

The use of computers has changed recordkeeping forever. A supercomputer can remember up to 250 million words at one time. In the past the U.S. government needed many rooms full of paper files. Today the same records can be stored in a small part of a computer memory. Computers can take in new information as fast as computer operators can put it in. The information is immediately organized and put into the right file in the computer. It can be printed out again in less than a second.

Every time you register in a school, get a driver's license or social security number, pay income tax, vote, register your car, apply for a passport or apply for a government job, the information is put into a government computer. All of this information about many people is called a data bank. A regular bank keeps many people's money in one place. A data bank keeps information about many people in one place.

Data banks are used at every level of government from small town government to the federal government in Washington, D.C.

When you apply for a passport, your name is put into a computer. Your name is checked against a list of many thousands of names. The government thinks the people on this list should not have a U.S. passport. Your name might be on the list if you have broken the law in some way. Without the computer, it would take a person a very long time to check all the names. The computer can do it in a few minutes. If there isn't anything bad about you in the data bank, you can get a passport.

Before you can get a job with the U.S. Defense Department, your name is put through the data banks of the FBI, CIA, Department of Defense, Civil Service, Immigration Service, and the House Committee on Internal Security. If any of these data banks has any bad information about you, you will not get the job.

Some people think the use of data banks is both good and bad. With information about people, the government can know where to build new schools, roads, airports, and parks. But many people do not want the government to know everything about them.

Check Your Guess

Directions: *You guessed the meaning of these words from this story. Circle the letter beside the answer that gives the same idea as the new word.*

1. When a computer is used correctly and when it is in good repair, it never makes a <u>mistake</u>.

   a. an answer

   b. a problem

   c. something wrong

2. Computers can pull out a single fact in an <u>instant</u> and never forget.

   a. a second

   b. the smallest amount of time

   c. a minute

3. The use of computers has changed recordkeeping <u>forever</u>.

   a. for all time

   b. for some time

   c. for a long time

Figure 47   A personal computer

4. Computers can take in new information as fast as computer <u>operators</u> can put it in.

   a. a person

   b. work

   c. tapes

5. Now every time you <u>register</u> in a school, the information is put in a computer.

   a. study

   b. sign forms to enter

   c. graduate

6. When you <u>apply</u> for a passport or <u>apply</u> for a government job, the information is put into a government computer.

   a. ask for in writing

   b. get

   c. pay for

Comprehension Exercises

Part 1: *You can find the answers to these questions in the story. You may look back to find an answer if you don't remember.*

1. How long have we had computers?

2. How fast is a computer?

3. How has the computer changed recordkeeping?

4. What is a data bank?

Part 2: *You may not find the answers to these questions in the story. You can answer the questions if you understand the ideas.*

1. How can you get your name on a U.S. government computer?

2. Explain what computer checks will be made if a person applies for a U.S. passport.

3. Explain what computer checks will be made on a person who wants to get a job with the U.S. Defense Department. Why is this so important?

Comprehension Check

Directions: *Read each sentence. Write T if it is true. Write F if it is false. Do not look back in the story.*

_____ 1. Computers are usually large.

_____ 2. Computers can forget.

_____ 3. Computers can solve almost any problem.

_____ 4. Computers can break down.

_____ 5. Computers can make mistakes.

_____ 6. Computers can find and print out information in less than a second.

_____ 7. You can get a U.S. passport if you have been in prison.

_____ 8. The fastest and best part of computer operation is the part that people do.

_____ 9. You can probably get a U.S. passport faster now than before computers.

_____ 10. The U.S. government probably has some information about every U.S. citizen.

Discussion Activities

Directions: *Discuss these topics as a class or in a small group.*

1. Why is the use of data banks good? Why is it bad?
2. Go to a place where a computer is in operation. Ask the computer operator to tell you what the computer can do and report back to the class.

   Some interesting field trips:

   —A large mainframe computer, perhaps at a university
   —A desktop publisher
   —Any government facility computer
   —A computer store where you can see the smallest computers
3. What do you think computers will be able to do in the future?

TIMED READING

Computers in Space

Directions: *Read quickly. Your teacher will time you. Put your reading rate on Chart 1 in the back of this book.*

People could not go into space without computers. Computers can	10
hold a lot of information. They solve many problems quickly in order to	23
bring people back safely to earth.	29
Apollo 13 was sent into space on April 11, 1970, with three	41
astronauts on board. They were on their way to the moon. The trip went	55
well for two days. When Apollo 13 was 200,000 miles away from earth,	68
there was a sudden problem. The spaceship was losing oxygen. The	79
men might die without enough oxygen before they could return to	90
earth.	91

Very quickly, the scientists in the Manned Spacecraft Center in 101
Houston, Texas, went to work on the problem. How could these men be 114
returned quickly and safely to earth? Would they have enough oxygen 125
left to return? 128

It would have taken months of work for scientists alone to study all 141
the possible answers to these problems. They could use only one 152
thing—a computer. One of the largest and fastest computers in the 164
world was at the Manned Spacecraft Center in Houston. 173

Scientists quickly thought up all possible ways to save the men in 185
Apollo 13. They put the information into the computer as fast as they 198
could. They did not stop to eat or rest. For 12 hours, scientists and the 213
computer worked without stopping. For every possible answer to the 223
problem, the computer told how long it would take, how much fuel, 235
how much oxygen, and the chances of success or failure. 245

Finally, the computer came up with the best answer. The three 256
astronauts came back to earth safely. They landed in the ocean only 268
one-half mile from the ship which picked them up. 277

This is an example of the importance of computers. The computer 288
actually saved the lives of the three astronauts. The computer found the 300
answer to the problem faster than scientists could. 308

The computer is so important to space travel that scientists do not 320
want the computer to break down when they need it. It is built to work 335
approximately six years without repair. The Spacecraft Center has a 345
second computer just like the first one. They can use the second 357
computer if there is any trouble with the first one. Computers are 369
necessary for a safe, successful trip into space. 377

Reading to Find Information

Directions: *Read the question. Then move your eyes over the paragraph that follows it. It is not necessary to read every word carefully. Just look for the answer to the question. Put a line under the answer. Work quickly.*

How far from earth was the spaceship when there was a problem?

Apollo 13 was sent into space on April 11, 1970, with three astronauts on board. They were on their way to the moon. The trip went well for two days. When Apollo 13 was 200,000 miles away from earth, there was a sudden problem. The spaceship was losing oxygen. The men might die without enough oxygen before they could return to earth.

What information did the computer tell?

Scientists quickly thought up all possible ways to save the men in Apollo 13. They put the information into the computer as fast as they could. They did not stop to eat or rest. For 12 hours, scientists and the computer worked without stopping. For every possible answer to the problem, the computer told how long it would take, how much fuel, how much oxygen, and the chances of success or failure.

Reading to Find the Main Idea

Directions: *Read the three titles. Then read the paragraph. Choose the title that is best for the whole paragraph.*

    a. A Computer That Works Six Years without Repair
    b. An Extra Computer at the Manned Spacecraft Center
    c. The Manned Spacecraft Center Must Not Be without a Computer

The computer is so important to space travel that scientists do not want the computer to break down when they need it. It is built to work approximately six years without repair. The Spacecraft Center has a second computer just like the first one. They can use the second computer if there is any trouble with the first one. Computers are necessary for a safe, successful trip into space.

Using the Context

Directions: *You don't always need to know all of the words in a story. You can still understand the ideas. Read the following paragraph or paragraphs. Don't worry about the blanks at first. Answer the true/false questions for all paragraphs. Then go back and fill in the blanks with a word you know.*

Finally, the computer came up with the best answer. The three astronauts came back to earth _____. They landed in the _____ only

₁   ₂

one-half mile from the ship which picked them up.

This is an example of the _____ of computers. The computer

                                                       ₃

_____ saved the lives of the three astronauts. The computer found the

₄

answer to the problem faster than scientists could.

_____ Even though there were problems, the spaceship made a perfect landing.

Timed Reading

Directions: *Read the timed reading again. Your teacher will time your reading. Put your reading rate on Chart 2 in the back of this book.*

Timed Reading Comprehension Check

Directions:
1. *Answer all the questions about the timed reading.*
2. *Go back to the timed reading and check your answers. Put a line under the answer in the timed reading. In the blank, write the line number where you found the answer in the timed reading.*
3. *When you have finished, your teacher may ask you to talk about the answers in a small group. In your group, try to agree on the answers, and then report back to the class.*

Line Number	*Answer*	*True/False:*
_____	_____	1. People die without oxygen.
_____	_____	2. Scientists could probably have found the way to bring the astronauts back to earth without a computer.
_____	_____	3. People can't go into space without computers.
_____	_____	4. One of the computers at the Manned Spacecraft Center is a little bit better than the other one.
_____	_____	5. The computer solved the simple problems, but the scientists solved the difficult problems.

Directions: *Choose one word from the list to put in each blank.*

apply	mistake
instant	operator
forever	register

1. If the scientists had made a _____, the astronauts might have died in space.

2. A computer can add, subtract, multiply, and divide in an _____.

3. The spacecraft, Pioneer 10, will probably travel in space _____.

4. The telephone _____ helped me make a long-distance call.

5. If I want to go to the university in the fall, I must _____ by January 30.

6. I will _____ for a scholarship. I hope I get it!

How Does a Computer Work?

Directions: *Your teacher may use this as a timed reading in class or let you read it by yourself outside of class.*

A computer can do many jobs at high speed. It can add, subtract,	13
multiply, and divide. It can compare numbers and decide which is	24
bigger and which is smaller. It can organize long lists of things in any	38
order. It can remember any number of facts, and it can bring these facts	52
back out of its memory and give them to its human users.	64

The first computers were very large and expensive. In the middle	75
1970s, microchips began to be used in computers. They are about as	87
small as your smallest fingernail. With microchips, computers are now	97
much smaller, 100 times faster, and 1000 times cheaper to run.	108

If you look at a microchip through a microscope, you can see that	121
each tiny chip is like a small city. There are rows and rows of wires that	137
look like streets on a city map. In a city, the traffic is controlled by traffic	153
lights. On a microchip, the electric signals are controlled by transistors.	164
The transistors are like a switch that can be on or off, like a light switch.	180
You use switches every day when you turn electric lights off and on in	194
your room. These thousands of transistors built into microchips act as	205
switches and make it possible for a computer to count and solve	217
problems for us.	220

Computers count electrically. To a computer, a switch that is on	231
represents a one. A switch that is off represents a zero. Because only two	245
digits or numbers are used, this is called a binary system. The word	258
binary means two.	261

To count like a computer, imagine a counter made of four lights in a	275
row. Each of these four lights has a number over it. Many computers use	289
the numbers 8, 4, 2, and 1.	296

Each light has a switch to turn it off or on. When a light is on, it	313
represents the number above it. When a light is off, it represents zero.	326

When all of the switches are off, all of the lights are off. The	340
computer counts zero.	343

To count 1, the switch under light 1 is turned on. The light turns	357
on, and the computer counts 1.	363

To count 2, the switch under light 1 is turned off. The switch under	377
light 2 is turned on. The light that represents 2 comes on. The computer	391
counts 2.	393

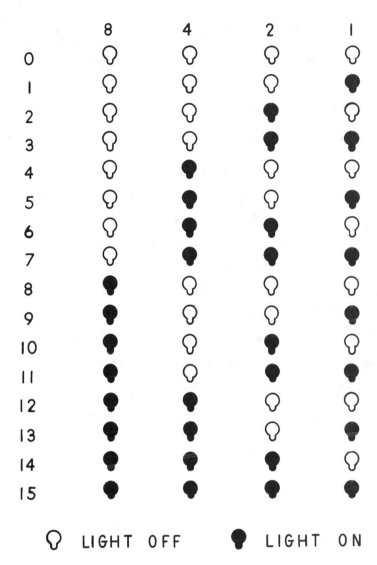

Figure 48 **A four switch counter made with four light bulbs**

To count 3, the switch under light 1 is turned on again. Now both the 2 and the 1 lights are on. The computer adds these together to get 3.

By using different combinations of the numbers 8, 4, 2, and 1, you need only four switches for the computer to add up to 15. By using more four-switch counters, computers can count up to very large numbers. With only 20 switches, a computer can count to over 1 million.

A computer made with microchips can count faster electrically than people can think. The electrical signals that pass through the microchip travel at nearly the speed of light. Each switch can go on or off

more than 1 million times in less than one second. This is why a   522
computer can solve almost any problem faster than people can.   532
Computers are one of the most important inventions of our time.   543

Comprehension Questions

Directions: *Read each sentence. Put T if it is true. Put F if it is false.*

_____ 1. A microchip is about the size of a quarter.

_____ 2. Computers can be smaller if they use microchips.

_____ 3. Microchips are expensive.

_____ 4. You can see the wires on a microchip with your eyes.

_____ 5. A transistor acts like a traffic light or a light switch.

_____ 6. Microchips were used in the middle 1960s.

_____ 7. In a microchip, electricity travels at the speed of light.

_____ 8. Each switch can go on or off 1 million times per minute.

_____ 9. A binary system uses the numbers 1 and 2.

_____ 10. A computer counts like people do.

chapter 15 _____

The Ocean Floor

Introduction

Directions: *Talk about these questions before you read the story.*

What oceans have you visited?

What is under the ocean?

Is the bottom of the ocean flat?

How deep is the ocean?

Why is the ocean important to us?

Directions: *Read the story quickly. Try to guess the meaning of new words. Don't use your dictionary.*

Almost three-fourths of the earth is under the ocean. Until a few years ago, people did not know what the ocean bottom, or floor, was like.

The ocean floor is different from what we thought. After World War I scientists made a new machine. This machine told them what the bottom of the ocean was like. The machine told how deep the ocean is in each place. For a long time many people thought the ocean floor was flat. Now we know that there are large mountains and deep holes in the ocean floor.

There are three kinds of ocean floor under the water: the continental shelf, the continental slope, and the deep ocean floor. The continental shelf goes all around the continents. (The continents are North America, South America, Europe, Australia, Asia, Africa, and Antarctica.) The water is not more than 600 feet deep above the continental shelf. The sun can shine only about 600 feet into the water. Plants and animals need sunshine to live. Most of the fish in the ocean live above the continental shelf.

The continental shelves were part of the continents many thousands of years ago. Later, the water came over them. Oil and minerals are in the continental shelf like they are in the land.

Oceanographers are scientists who study the oceans. They think the continental shelves will be very important to us someday. They are trying to learn how to live and work under the water at 500 feet or more. Then they can get some of the oil and minerals that are located there.

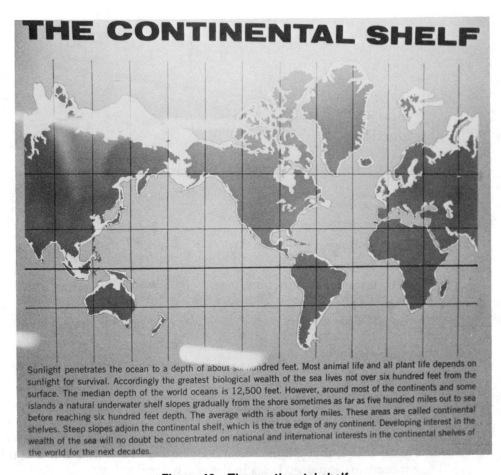

THE CONTINENTAL SHELF

Sunlight penetrates the ocean to a depth of about six hundred feet. Most animal life and all plant life depends on sunlight for survival. Accordingly the greatest biological wealth of the sea lives not over six hundred feet from the surface. The median depth of the world oceans is 12,500 feet. However, around most of the continents and some islands a natural underwater shelf slopes gradually from the shore sometimes as far as five hundred miles out to sea before reaching six hundred feet depth. The average width is about forty miles. These areas are called continental shelves. Steep slopes adjoin the continental shelf, which is the true edge of any continent. Developing interest in the wealth of the sea will no doubt be concentrated on national and international interests in the continental shelves of the world for the next decades.

Figure 49   The continental shelf

The continental slope begins where the continental shelf ends. At the edge of the continental shelf, the continental slope suddenly goes down two or three miles. Some continental slopes are like the side of a mountain; some are like a wall. All are very high. The largest one is five miles high. This is higher than any slope on land. There are large canyons in the continental slopes. The canyons look like the Grand Canyon, but they are larger.

The deep ocean floor begins at the end of the continental slope. It is the real bottom of the ocean. It is the largest and deepest of the three kinds of ocean bottom. The deep ocean floor makes up half of all the earth's surface.

Oceanographers have found a large range, or line, of mountains called the Mid-Atlantic Ridge on the ocean floor. This mountain range is 10,000 miles long. It goes through the Atlantic Ocean from Iceland to southern Africa. Many of the mountains in this range are 10,000 feet high. The Atlantic Ocean is very deep. It covers mountains 10,000 feet high with a mile or more of water. However, a few mountains in the Mid-Atlantic Ridge are even higher. We can see their tops above the ocean surface. The Azore Islands, near Portugal, are really the tops of some of these mountains.

The Pacific Ocean has large mountains, too. The Hawaiian Islands are tops of mountains 32,000 feet high. There are some large, long holes in the ocean bottom called trenches. One of the deepest is near New Zealand. This trench is seven miles deep and is 1,600 miles long. It is big enough to hold six Grand Canyons.

Now we know that there are mountains, canyons, and trenches under the ocean. Soon people will be able to live and work on the continental shelves. However, it will be a long time before people will be able to go to the deep ocean floor.

Check Your Guess

Directions: *You guessed the meaning of these words from this story. Circle the letter beside the answer that gives the same idea as the new word. Do not use a dictionary.*

1. Until a few years ago, people didn't know what the ocean bottom, or <u>floor</u>, was like.

    a. water

    b. rug

    c. bottom

2. Oceanographers have found a large <u>range</u>, or line, of mountains called the Mid-Atlantic Ridge on the ocean floor.

    a. line

    b. rock

    c. stone

3. The continental shelves were part of the continents many thousands of years ago. Later, the water came over them. Oil and <u>minerals</u> are in the continental shelf like they are in the land.

Which is a mineral?

a. fish

b. gold

c. plants

4. There are some large, long holes in the ocean bottom called <u>trenches</u>.

a. fish

b. holes

c. plants

5. The Azore <u>Islands</u>, near Portugal, are really the tops of some of these mountains.

a. land with water all around it

b. water with land all around it

c. water near land

Comprehension Exercises

Part 1: *You can find the answers to these questions in the story. You may look back to find an answer if you don't remember.*

1. How much of the earth is under the oceans?

2. What are the three kinds of ocean bottom?

3. How deep is the water above the continental shelf?

4. What can you find in or above the continental shelf?

5. Where is the Mid-Atlantic Ridge?

6. How high are some mountains in the Pacific Ocean?

7. How deep is one trench? Where is it?

Part 2: *You may not find the answers to these questions in the story. You can answer the questions if you understand the ideas in the story.*

1. Why didn't people know what the ocean bottom was like before?

2. Why do most of the fish in the ocean live above the continental shelves?

3. Do you think there are plants on the deep ocean floor? Why?

4. Why do you think oil and minerals are in the continental shelves?

5. About how deep is the Atlantic Ocean?

6. Look at Figure 50. Which two continents are joined by the continental shelf?

Comprehension Check

Directions: *Read each sentence. Write T if it is true. Write F if it is false. Do not look back in the story.*

_____ 1. New Zealand is a continent.

_____ 2. We have known for hundreds of years what the ocean floor is like.

_____ 3. The continental shelf is the deepest part of the ocean.

_____ 4. The continental shelves were part of the continents thousands of years ago.

_____ 5. The continental slope is the real bottom of the ocean.

_____ 6. The Mid-Atlantic Ridge goes from North America to Europe.

_____ 7. Some mountains in the Mid-Atlantic Ridge are more than 15,000 feet high.

_____ 8. The largest mountains in the oceans are in the Atlantic Ocean.

_____ 9. New Zealand is really the top of some mountains.

_____ 10. The trench near New Zealand is bigger than the Grand Canyon.

Discussion Activities

Directions: *Discuss these topics in class or in a small group.*

1. Find these things on a world map. Show them to the class.
   a. the oceans
   b. the continents
   c. the Azore Islands
   d. the Hawaiian Islands
   e. New Zealand
   f. the Mid-Atlantic Ridge
   g. the equator
   h. the Gulf Stream

2. Why is it important to study the bottom of the ocean?

3. Describe the continental slope.

TIMED READING

The Continents

Directions: *Read quickly. Your teacher will time you. Put your reading rate on Chart 1 in the back of this book.*

Scientists take all the ideas they know about something. They try	11
to put them all together into a theory. A theory is someone's idea of how	26
something may have happened. A theory is not certain. When scientists	37
find out something new, they have to change their theories. This is what	50
happened to their theories about how the continents were made.	60
Around 1915, a man named Alfred Wegener suggested a theory	70
about the continents. He saw that the continents looked like they could	82
go together. He said that in the beginning there was only one continent.	95
This large continent was around the South Pole. Wegener thought that	106
the continent broke into seven pieces about 300 million years ago. The	118
pieces drifted* to the places where they are now. As they moved, they	131
pushed up mountains. He called this theory *continental drift*.	140
After World War II, scientists began to learn more and more about	152
the bottom of the ocean. They had to change all their theories about how	166
the continents were made.	170
Scientists made some new machines to make a map of the ocean	182
floor. They learned how deep the ocean is in each place. They made	195
machines to take people down to the ocean floor. Under the ocean, they	208
found a new mountain range which they called the Mid-Atlantic Ridge.	219

*drift–to move along without knowing where one is going

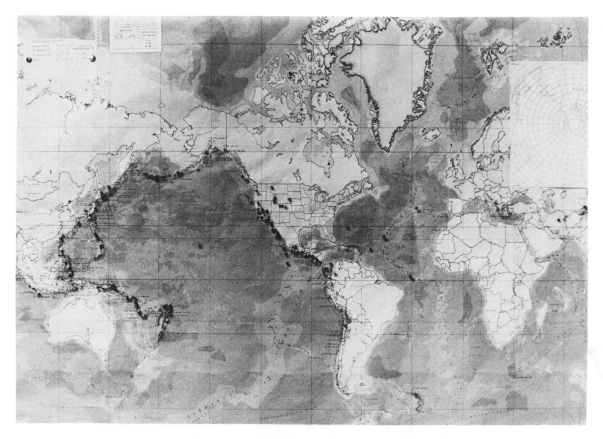

Figure 50 Where earthquakes happen

They learned that there are a lot of earthquakes in those mountains.   231
Earthquakes happen when something makes the earth move.   239

　　With some of their machines, scientists also brought up some of   250
the dirt from the ocean floor. They were very surprised at what they   263
found. They knew that the earth was 4 or 5 billion years old. They found   278
that the dirt on the ocean floor was only about 80 million years old. They   293
began to think that something happened to change the ocean floor about   305
100 million years ago.   309

　　A scientist named Hess formulated another theory about the   318
continents. He called the theory *plate tectonics*. He proposed this theory   329
after he studied a map which showed where all the earthquakes   340
happened between 1963 and 1977. The earthquake lines on the map   351
divided the earth into eight parts. Hess's theory says that eight large   363
<u>plates</u>* make up the outside of the earth. These plates are always   375

*plate—a flat surface

moving, but not very fast. They move at speeds of from half an inch to 390
six inches a year. At places where the plates meet, earthquakes can 402
happen. Mountains can be pushed up where the plates meet. Dirt from 414
the ocean floor can fall down between the plates. Scientists can know 426
where earthquakes will happen in the future—at places where the plates 438
meet. 439

Scientists now think that there was only one large continent until 450
about 200 million years ago. Then the eight plates began moving very 462
slowly. It took about 145 million years for the seven continents to break 475
away from each other. It took 55 million years more for them to get 489
where they are now. 493

As scientists learn more about the land and the ocean floor, they 505
may have to change their theory again. 512

READING SKILLS EXERCISES

Reading to Find Information

Directions: *Read the question. Then move your eyes over the paragraph that follows it. It is not necessary to read every word carefully. Just look for the answer to the question. Put a line under the answer. Work quickly.*

How big is the trench near New Zealand?

The Pacific Ocean has large mountains too. The Hawaiian Islands are tops of mountains 32,000 feet high. There are some large, long holes in the ocean bottom called trenches. One of the deepest is near New Zealand. This trench is seven miles deep and is 1,600 miles long. It is big enough to hold six Grand Canyons.

How old is the earth?

With some of their machines, scientists also brought up some of the dirt from the ocean floor. They were very surprised at what they found. They knew that the earth was 4 or 5 billion years old. They found that the dirt on the ocean floor was only about 80 million years old. They began to think that something happened to change the ocean floor about 100 million years ago.

Reading to Find the Main Idea

Directions: *Read the three titles. Then read the paragraph. Choose the title that is best for the whole paragraph.*

a. What a Theory Is

b. Where Scientists Get Theories
c. How to Change a Theory

Scientists take all the ideas they know about something. They try to put them all together into a theory. A theory is someone's idea of how something may have happened. A theory is not certain. When scientists find out something new, they have to change their theories. This is what happened to their theories about how the continents were made.

Using the Context

Directions: *You don't always need to know all of the words in a story. You can still understand the ideas. Read the following paragraph or paragraphs. Don't worry about the blanks at first. Answer the true/false questions for all paragraphs. Then go back and fill in the blanks with a word you know.*

The ocean floor is _____ from what we thought. After World War I, scientists made a new machine. This _____ _____ told them what the bottom of the _____ __ was like. The machine told how _____ the ocean is in each place. For a long time _____ people thought the ocean floor was flat. Now we know that _____ are large mountains and deep holes in the ocean floor.

_____ We know how deep the ocean is.

Timed Reading

Directions: *Read the timed reading again. Your teacher will time your reading. Put your reading rate on Chart 2 in the back of this book.*

Timed Reading Comprehension Check

Directions: 1. *Answer all the questions about the timed reading.*
2. *Go back to the timed reading and check your answers. Put a line under the answer in the timed reading. In the blank, write the line number where you found the answer in the timed reading.*
3. *When you have finished, your teacher may ask you to talk about the answers in a small group. In your group, try to agree on the answers, and then report back to the class.*

Line Number	Answer	True/False:
_____	_____	1. A theory is true.
_____	_____	2. Before World II, scientists did not know much about the ocean floor.
_____	_____	3. The ocean floor is flat.
_____	_____	4. Sometimes there are earthquakes under the ocean.
_____	_____	5. The dirt on the ocean floor is as old as the earth.
_____	_____	6. Hess's theory says there are eight plates under the earth.
_____	_____	7. The plates move very fast.
_____	_____	8. Scientists can know where earthquakes will happen in the future.
_____	_____	9. Scientists will never again change their theories about the continents.
_____	_____	10. The earth is 4 or 5 billion years old.

Directions: *Choose one word from the list to put in each blank.*

earthquakes	plates
drift	theory
trenches	islands
floor	range
machine	minerals

1. We learned what the ocean _____ is like from a _____.

2. Many mountains in this large _____ are 10,000 feet high.

3. If we learn to live and work under the water, we can get the _____ that are on the continental shelf.

4. One of the deepest _____ is near New Zealand.

5. The Hawaiian _____ are tops of mountains 32,000 feet high.

We Share the Earth

Directions: *Your teacher may use this as a timed reading in class or let you read it by yourself outside of class.*

In recent years, there has been a great deal of interest in Ecology,   13
the science of the relationship between living things and their   23
environment. Human beings have no control over events of nature such   34
as snow, rain, and lightning. However, there are many things that   45
happen in the environment that are under the control of, or caused by,   58
people. It is possible in the near future that people may cause enough   71
harm to the environment to change the climate of the earth forever.   83

HELP! I'M LOSING MY BALANCE!

Figure 51

There is always a layer of gases around the earth which we call the   97
atmosphere. Like a blanket, this layer makes the earth warm enough for   109
life and provides the air we breathe. Earth is the only one of all the   124
planets we know about which has the right temperature for life as we   137
know it. If the climate becomes too hot or too cold, life on earth cannot 152
continue to exist. Therefore, scientists are studying two theories: the   162
possibility of the *greenhouse effect* and the possibility of a *nuclear winter*. 174
Both possibilities may result in a major change in the ecology of the   187
earth, the balance between man and nature.   194

A greenhouse is a house made of glass. The sun shines right   206
through the glass and makes it warm inside the greenhouse. It is   218
possible to grow flowers and vegetables inside a greenhouse in the   229
winter. Scientists have a theory that a lot of carbon dioxide in the   242
atmosphere will act like the glass in a greenhouse. As the sun shines   255
through the carbon dioxide *blanket*, the atmosphere will get hotter and   266
hotter. Scientists predict that as a result of more carbon dioxide in the 279
atmosphere, there will be a global warming, or a long-term rise in   291
temperatures over the earth.   295

Carbon dioxide is produced by combustion, the burning of fuel. It   306
is being added to the normal atmosphere as we have more and more   319
cars, more and more houses to heat, and more industries. In short, more   332
people produce more carbon dioxide.   337

Scientists can predict the results of a global warming. The ice will   349
melt at the North and South Poles. If this happens, ocean levels will rise 363
and flood cities like New York and Los Angeles on the coasts of   376
continents. The centers of large continents such as North America will   387
be come hotter and drier. There will be severe droughts in the Midwest   400
of the United States. The weather will be very hot, and there will not be 415
enough rain. The drought will destroy crops like corn and wheat. The   427
effects on agriculture and the world economy will be great. Some   438
scientists predict that the possibility of a severe drought will increase 449
from the 3 to 5 percent chance we have now to 60 percent by the year   465
2150.   466

The possibility of nuclear winter from atomic war might produce   476
similar effects on the ecology. Scientists predict that if there is a nuclear 489
war, the result will be that everyone will die, either immediately from   501
the bombs or later from the results of a nuclear winter.   512

In 1982, some scientists gave the name nuclear winter to their idea   524
of what would happen after a nuclear war. They predict a nuclear winter   537
will be like this: The explosion of atomic bombs would result in a great   551
amount of dust and smoke from fires, which would block out the sun   564
and result in the cooling of the earth. A nuclear war would kill many   578
people, but most of the population would die afterwards from lack of   590

food. Many scientists think cold darkness would blanket the earth and make it impossible to grow crops.

To support their theory, scientists show the example of what happened in California in 1988. Eighty square miles of trees burned for over a month in California and Oregon. In some places in those states, temperatures dropped from 9 to 30 degrees Farenheit lower than normal for a three-week period because the smoke blocked the sunlight.

The drop in temperature would be much greater in a nuclear winter. Some people think that fires from bombs would burn more than 80,000 square miles of forest. There would also be more smoke from the burning of industrial plants and oil refineries.

Everyone who lives on the earth must make some decisions about the possible greenhouse effect and nuclear winter. As the population of the world grows, we must be more careful about the effect our "progress" is having on the earth. The countries of the world must work together to protect the environment and to live in peace because we share the earth.

Directions: *Read each sentence. Write I if it is true. Write F if it is false.*

_____ 1. The *greenhouse effect* and *nuclear winter* are theories.
_____ 2. All scientists agree that global warming is a fact.
_____ 3. Carbon dioxide is good for people.
_____ 4. Drought is good for corn and wheat.
_____ 5. Ecology is the study of the balance between man and nature.
_____ 6. A drought means hot temperatures and a lot of rain.
_____ 7. New York City and Los Angeles are coastal cities.
_____ 8. The greenhouse effect might result in a global cooling.
_____ 9. A nuclear winter might result in lower temperatures.
_____ 10. A blanket is a cover.

chapter 16 _____

The Grand Canyon

Introduction

Directions: *Talk about these questions before you read the story.*

Look at the picture of the Grand Canyon.
Have you ever visited the Grand Canyon? Tell the class about it.
Where is the Grand Canyon? Show the class on a map.
What is unusual about the Grand Canyon?
Why do people want to visit it?

Directions: *Read the story quickly. Try to guess the meaning of new words. Don't use your dictionary.*

Every year many people go to see the Grand Canyon in Arizona. In the last 10 million years, the Colorado River has cut down into the earth there. It has made a beautiful canyon about one mile deep.

Geologists are scientists who study rocks. They are very interested in the Grand Canyon. They look at the different layers and colors of earth and rock in the canyon walls. They can see how the earth has changed as it has grown older.

We can't see the layers of earth and rock in other places because they are under the ground. Sometimes the layers are flat; sometimes they are not. The oldest layer is on the bottom. A newer layer is above it. The newest layer is on the top. They are like a lot of papers on top of each other. The one on the bottom was put down first. The second from the bottom was put down next. The top one was put down last. Geologists look at the layers of earth from the bottom to the top. They can see what happened to the earth in that place.

Figure 52   The Grand Canyon

Scientists can see a story of 2 billion years of earth history in the rocks of the Grand Canyon. When they look down a mile into the canyon, they are looking back in time.

In the beginning the earth was hot everywhere. Then about 2 billion years ago, the earth became cooler. The outside of the earth became a little smaller as it became cooler. This made large mountains in the place where the Grand Canyon is now. Some lava came to the surface, and the rocks became very hard. There was no life of any kind on earth—no grass, trees, or animals. You can see dark rocks at the bottom of the Grand Canyon from this time.

For the next billion years, the wind and rain eroded these mountains until they were almost flat again. Then the ocean came over this place. The water moved dirt, sand, and rocks into the place where the Grand Canyon is now. The dirt, sand, and rocks were heavier than the water. They slowly went down to the bottom of the water. They became sediment. The water pushed hard on them until they became sedimentary rock. The ocean made thousands of feet of sedimentary rock in this place.

This story is repeated in the rocks at the Grand Canyon at least three times. Three more times the earth pushed mountains up. Three more times the wind and rain eroded the mountains. Three more times the ocean came over the land. The ocean put down more layers of sedimentary rock. The ocean left fish and plants in that rock.

About 10 million years ago, the land around the Grand Canyon began to push upward. The land was higher and drier than before. The Colorado River began to run faster. It began to cut the Grand Canyon.

Today you can go to see 2 billion years of history at the Grand Canyon. It was made by nature, not by humans.

Check Your Guess

Directions: *You guessed the meaning of these words from this story. Circle the letter beside the answer that gives the same idea as the new word.*

1. They look at the different <u>layers</u> and colors of earth and rock in the canyon walls.

   a. lines   b. mountains   c. papers

2. The dirt, sand, and rocks were <u>heavier</u> than the water. They slowly went down to the bottom of the water. This is <u>sediment</u>.

   a. more air
   b. more weight
   c. more layers

   a. lava
   b. layers
   c. heavy things that go to the bottom of water

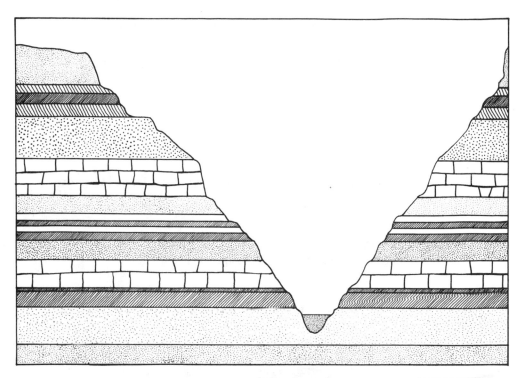

Figure 53 Layers at the Grand Canyon

3. For the next billion years, the wind and rain <u>eroded</u> these mountains.

   a. washed away   b. pushed up   c. fell on

4. This story is <u>repeated</u> three more times. Three more times the earth pushed mountains up. Three more times the wind and rain <u>eroded</u> the mountains. Three more times the ocean came over the land.

   a. pushed again   b. done again   c. washed again

5. Sometimes the layers are <u>flat</u>; sometimes they are not.

   a. short, not long   b. cool, not hot   c. smooth, not up and down

Comprehension Exercises

Part 1: *You can find the answers to these questions in the story. You may look back to find an answer if you don't remember.*

1. Who studies rocks?

2. What do the different layers and colors of rocks tell us?

3. How old are the oldest rocks at the bottom of the canyon?

4. What is sediment?

5. How does the ocean make sedimentary rock?

6. When did the Colorado River begin to cut the Grand Canyon?

Part 2: *You may not find the answers to these questions in the story. You can answer the questions if you undersatnd the ideas in the story.*

1. Explain why the oldest layer of earth is at the bottom. Use your own words. Compare the layers to a lot of papers on top of each other.

2. Explain how the wind, rain, and ocean changed the land where the Grand Canyon is now.

3. Why do you think geologists are interested in the Grand Canyon?

4. Look at Figure 54. What kinds of life can be found at the Grand Canyon in rocks 230 million years old? 65 million years old? 2 billion years old? How long have human beings been there?

Comprehension Check

Directions: *Read each sentence. Write T if it is true. Write F if it is false. Do not look back in the story.*

_____ 1. The Grand Canyon is in New Mexico.

_____ 2. Different layers of earth and rock are everywhere.

_____ 3. The oldest layers are on top.

_____ 4. The top layers were put down first.

_____ 5. The dark, hard rocks at the bottom of the Grand Canyon were made from lava.

_____ 6. The rocks at the bottom are a billion years old.

Name of Period	Type of Rock	Age	Kinds of Life Found in Rock
Cenozoic	volcanic	5,000 years 1 million years	human beings camels, mammoths
Mesozoic	conglomerate	65 million years	dinosaur tracks reptiles
Paleozoic	sandstone shale limestone	230 million years	sea animals, shark teeth, reptiles, worms, ferns, insects, four-footed animals, shellfish
Late Precambrian	quartzite shale limestone	600 million years	simple plant life
Early Precambrian	vishnu schist (volcanic)	2 billion years	no signs of life

Figure 54   Kinds of life found in the rock at the Grand Canyon

_____ 7. The ocean came over the land three times.

_____ 8. The Colorado River began to cut the Grand Canyon about 2 billion years ago.

_____ 9. Layers are always flat.

_____ 10. There are thousands of feet of sedimentary rock at the Grand Canyon.

Discussion Activities

Directions: *Discuss these topics as a class or in a small group.*

1. Humans didn't make the beautiful Grand Canyon; nature did. We want to keep it like it is for people to see in the future. Can you think of ways human beings might do something bad to the Grand Canyon? How might they change it so that it won't be as beautiful in the future?

2. The Grand Canyon is called one of the natural wonders of the world. What does this mean? Can you think of any other natural wonders of the world? Are there any in your country?

3. Why is the Grand Canyon important to us?

TIMED READING

How the Colorado River Made the Grand Canyon

Directions: *Read quickly. Your teacher will time you. Put your reading rate on Chart 1 in the back of this book.*

The Colorado River begins in Colorado, in Rocky Mountain	9
National Park. It goes 1,450 miles through Colorado, Utah, and Arizona	20
into the Gulf of California. How did the Colorado River cut the Grand	33
Canyon out of the earth?	38
The river goes down 10,000 feet from its highest point in the	50
mountains to sea level. It is narrow and very fast. The Colorado River	63
carries a lot of dirt, sand, and rocks in the water as it goes down the	79
mountains. These things help the river cut through the earth.	89
Sometimes the color of the river is red because there is so much sand	103
and rock in it. The river got its name from *Rio Colorado*, which is Spanish	118
for red river. The river has carried about a billion pounds of sand and	132
rock every day for many years.	138

Most people don't know how much a billion pounds is. To help   150
you see how much it is, here is a story. Try to think of a billion pounds of   168
dirt and sand in large trucks. To move a billion pounds of dirt and sand,   183
you would need 100,000 trucks. One truck must go by every second for   196
24 hours. The Colorado River moves this much dirt and sand in the   209
water every day.   212

Scientists think that the Colorado River cuts down into the earth   223
about six inches every thousand years. They think it took 10 million   235
years for the river to make the Grand Canyon. The Grand Canyon is one   249
mile deep now. It may grow almost half a mile deeper in the next million   264
years because the river is still half a mile above sea level. When the   278
canyon reaches sea level, the river will no longer cut down into the   291
land.   292

Part of the Grand Canyon is a national park 52 miles long and 22   306
miles wide.   308

READING SKILLS EXERCISES

Reading to Find Information

Directions: *Read the question. Then move your eyes over the paragraph that follows it. It is not necessary to read every word carefully. Just look for the answer to the question. Put a line under the answer. Work quickly.*

Which states does the Colorado River go through?

The Colorado River begins in Colorado, in Rocky Mountain National Park. It goes 1,450 miles through Colorado, Utah, and Arizona into the Gulf of California.

Reading to Find the Main Idea

Directions: *Read the three titles. Then read the paragraph. Choose the title that is best for the whole paragraph.*

   a.   How Far the River Cuts over a Period of Time
   b.   How Deep the Grand Canyon Is Now
   c.   How Far the River Will Cut in the Future

Scientists think that the Colorado River cuts down into the earth about six inches every thousand years. They think it took 10 million years for the river to make the Grand Canyon. The Grand Canyon is one mile deep now. It may grow almost half a mile deeper in the next million years because the river is still half a mile above sea level. When the canyon reaches sea level, the river will no longer cut down into the land.

Using the Context

Directions: *You don't always need to know all of the words in a story. You can still understand the ideas. Read the following paragraph or paragraphs. Don't worry about the blanks at first. Answer the true/false questions for all paragraphs. Then go back and fill in the blanks with a word you know.*

The river goes down 10,000 feet from its _____ point in the
1
mountains down to sea level. It is narrow and very _____. The
2
Colorado River carries a lot of dirt, _____, and rocks in the water
3
as it goes down the mountains. These help the _____ cut through the
4
earth.

_____ The Colorado River begins at the sea.

A few years ago, some people wanted to _____ a dam near the
1
Grand Canyon. The dam would make a lot of electricity. This was needed by the
growing population of _____. However, the dam would cover
2
_____ of the land near the Grand Canyon with water. Many people
3
against the dam. They wanted to _____ the Grand Canyon as it is for
4
future people to see and to study. It was an example of a fight between progress
and conservation. Which side do you agree with?

_____ A dam can make electricity.

Timed Reading

Directions: *Read the timed reading again. Your teacher will time your reading. Put your reading rate on Chart 2 in the back of this book.*

Timed Reading Comprehension Check

Directions: 1. *Answer all the questions about the timed reading.*
2. *Go back to the timed reading and check your answers. Put a line under the answer in the timed reading. In the blank, write the line number where you found the answer in the timed reading.*
3. *When you have finished, your teacher may ask you to talk about the answers in a small group. In your group, try to agree on the answers and then report back to the class.*

Line
Number   *Answer*

_____   _____   1. The Colorado River goes through
a. New Mexico.
b. Nevada.
c. Arizona.
d. all of the above.

True/False:

_____   _____   2. The Colorado River goes through two national parks.

_____   _____   3. In the future the Grand Canyon may be three miles deep.

_____   _____   4. Sometimes the Colorado River is red.

_____   _____   5. The Colorado River begins 10,000 feet above sea level.

Directions: *Choose one word from the list to put in each blank.*

flat	layers
repeated	eroded
heavier	sediment

1. Scientists can see a story of 2 billion years of earth's history in the _____ of the canyon.

2. _____ is _____ than water.

3. The wind and rain _____ the mountains at the Grand Canyon three times.

4. The history of the layers of rock is _____ in the canyon walls.

5. The wind and rain washed away the mountains until they were _____.

Volcanoes

Directions: *Your teacher may use this as a timed reading in class or let you read it by yourself outside of class.*

Scientists do not know how the earth was made. They have some 12
different theories about it. However, they agree that when the earth was 24
made, it was very hot. In the beginning, it was all <u>melted</u>* rock. The 38
rock was very different from the rock we know today. 48

After millions of years, the earth began to cool and become hard. 60
As the rock on the outside surface of the earth cooled, it started to make 75
a thin <u>crust</u>.† Many times the crust broke open, and the hot rock came 89
out to the earth's surface again. 95

After millions of years, the crust finally became hard. There were 106
dark clouds all around the earth, but it didn't rain while the earth was so 121
hot. The earth finally cooled enough so that rain could fall on its surface. 135
It rained and rained. Maybe it rained for years. The rain began to make 149
the oceans. 151

At the same time that the earth's crust cooled and became strong, 163
the inside of the earth stayed hot. Today, the hot rock inside the earth is 178
still melted. Magma is the name of the hot, thick, melted rock when it is 193
inside the earth. When it comes through holes to the surface, we call it 207
lava. 208

Underground magma makes mountains in two ways. As the 217
magma pushes up, it pushes on the earth's crust. In some places the 230
crust is strong. The magma can't break through so it pushes all of the 244
crust up. This makes mountains. Magma can push up to make 255
mountains where two plates meet. 260

Magma makes a mountain in another way when it finds a thin spot 273
in the crust. It makes a hole. Then suddenly, rocks, dirt, and lava fly 287
hundreds of feet into the air. This makes a lot of noise, shakes and 301
moves the earth, and can be very dangerous. This is a volcano. As the 315
rocks, dirt, and lava fall back onto the earth, they make a mountain 328
around the hole. About 400 volcanoes in the world today sometimes put 340
out lava. 342

*melted—changed from solid to liquid by heat. For example, when ice melts, it becomes
water.
†crust—any hard covering on the outside of something; for example, crust on the outside
of bread.

Figure 55   A volcano

Comprehension Check

Directions: *Choose the correct answer. Write the letter in the blank.*

_____   1. Magma makes mountains in places where
        a. the crust is strong.
        b. it finds a thin spot.
        c. two plates meet.
        d. all of the above.

        True/False:

_____   2. Scientists know how the earth was made.

_____   3. In the beginning, the earth was very hot.

_____   4. The hot rock inside the earth is still melted today.

_____   5. Magma and lava are the same thing.

_____   6. Today, about 1,000 volcanoes put out lava.

_____   7. Oceans were always on the earth.

_____   8. Mountains are made by underground magma.

_____   9. The earth developed as it is in a short time.

_____   10. Volcanoes can kill people.

Across

2. Causing strong feelings or goosebumps
4. What folds in the brain are called
7. Usual, middle
8. Trade
9. Letters and packages carried by a postal service
11. Take air into the body
12. A person who asks questions
14. To put something in the brain so you can remember it when you want to
17. These result when something doubles up on itself.
18. When married people legally end their marriage
20. He talks and listens to people to help them
22. To hold ideas in one's mind; to think or suppose
24. Paper money
26. Sure
27. The state when a person can't think, speak, or hear

Down

1. Describing something that costs a lot of money
3. To think in pictures
4. The thinking brain
5. To put in order, arrange
6. People working or playing together
10. Kind of bomb used in a war
13. A person sitting on a horse
15. The part of the brain that gets and sends information
16. Do the same thing again and again
19. Meaning, worth
21. The small parts of a picture or of an idea
23. The middle or most important part
25. What happens when two cars hit each other

185

Appendix 1 _____

Use the charts on the following pages to record how your reading rate progresses. Take the number at the end of the line where you stopped reading. Divide this number by the number of minutes you read. The answer is your rate of reading speed, or words per minute (w.p.m.). On the chart, under the number of the reading, find the line that shows the w.p.m. you read. Put a dot where the two lines meet. Do this for each timed reading and then connect the dots (see the sample chart below). The line will show your progress.

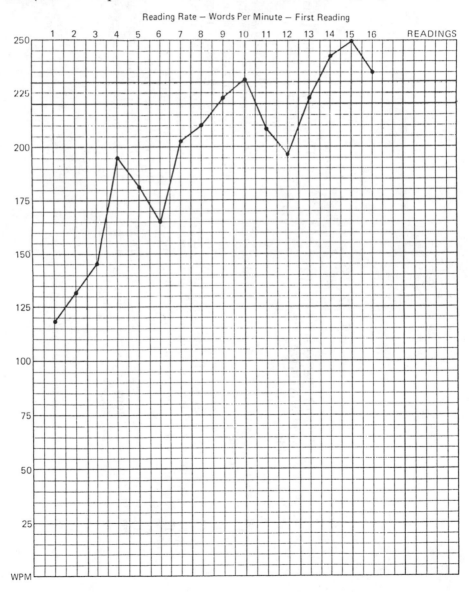

Reading Rate — Words Per Minute — First Reading

Reading Rate — Words Per Minute — First Reading

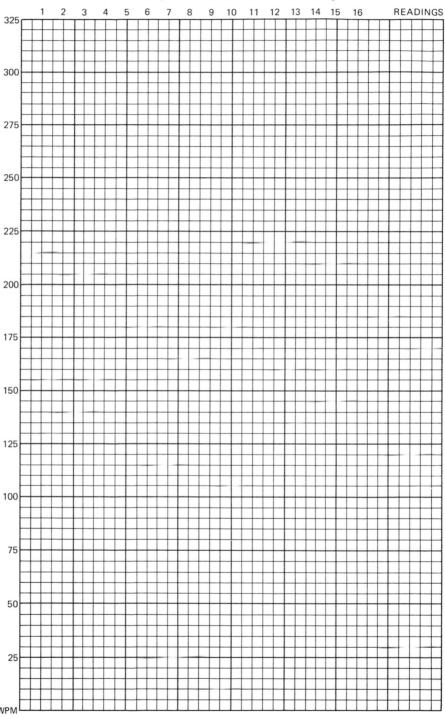

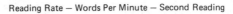
Reading Rate — Words Per Minute — Second Reading

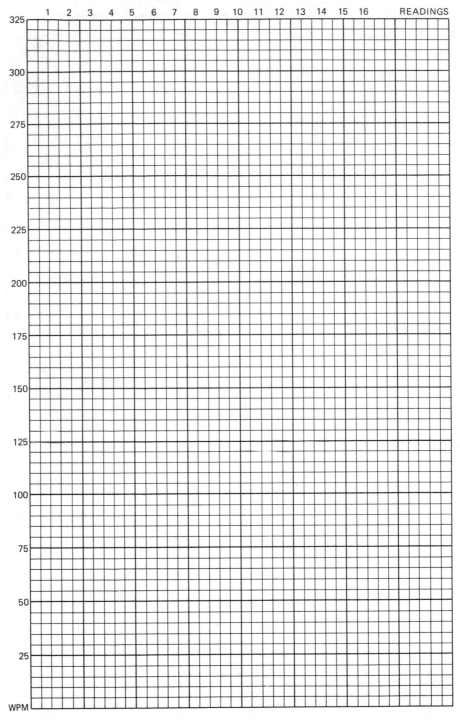

Reading Rate — Words Per Minute — Supplemental Readings

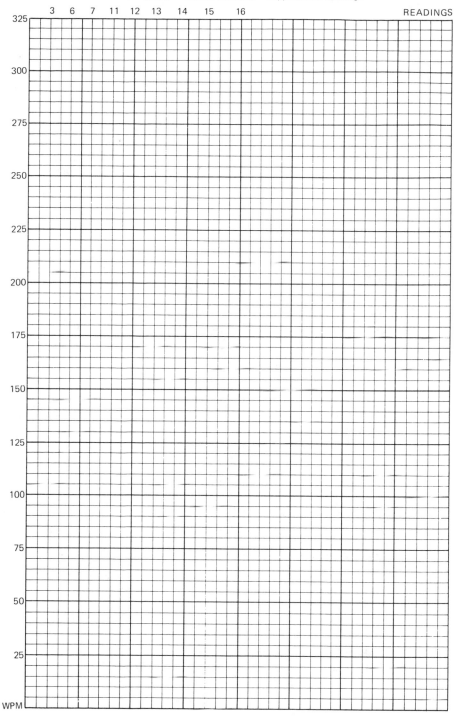

Appendix 2 _____

Modal Auxiliaries

Some modal auxiliaries are: can, could, must, should, may, might, and will. Auxiliary means *helper*. A modal auxiliary is a helping verb. The simple form of the main verb follows a modal auxiliary.

Basic Form	Negative Form	Question Form
He can do it.	He can't do it.	Can he do it?
She could do it.	She couldn't do it.	Could she do it?
He may do it.	He may not do it.	May he do it?
She might do it.	She might not do it.	Might she do it?
They must do it.	They must not do it.	Must they do it?
They should do it.	They shouldn't do it.	Should they do it?
He will do it.	He won't do it.	Will he do it?

	Meaning

1. Modals that say ability (able to do something).
    a. Some people can sleep better than other people.
    b. I could sleep better when I was young.
    c. We can go to the moon in 50 years.
	can = able to (present)
	could = able to (future)
	
	can = able to (future)

2. Modals that say advisability (that something is a good idea). a. The doctors thought they should let her die.	
3. Modals that say strong necessity (that something strongly needs to be done). a. We must try not to have an atomic war.	must is stronger than should

4. Modals that say possibility.
    a. In the future we may use hypnotism more than we do now.
    b. Hypnotism might be useful to you.
    c. We could use our thumbprints for money.	

5. Modals that say something is in the future. a. In thousands of years, the Grand Canyon will be deeper than it is now.	

Practice with Modals

Use must, should, may, might, can, could, or will in the following sentences. More than one word may be correct in some of the sentences.

1. We _____ go to other planets some day.
2. We _____ study for the test tomorrow.
3. They _____ not go because they didn't have a car.
4. Many scientists _____ study the ocean currents to get more information.
5. All people _____ work to stop atomic war.
6. What _____ you do after school?
7. I don't know if I _____ be hypnotized.

Reading Numbers

```
          millions   hundreds   ones
        ⌒⌒⌒              ↘        ↙
0  0  0 ,  0  0  0,  0  0  0,  0  0  0
⌣⌣⌣                ⌣⌣⌣      ↑
billions           thousands  tens
```

You read the number 59: fifty-nine.

You read the number 859: eight hundred fifty-nine.

You read the number 3,859: three thousand, eight hundred fifty-nine.

You read the number 63,859: sixty-three thousand, eight hundred fifty-nine.

You read the number 463,859: four hundred and sixty-three thousand, eight hundred fifty-nine.

Now, you read the following numbers:
6,463,859
76,463,859
176,463,859
5,176,463,859
65,176,463,859
265,176,463,859

Write these numbers:

1. One hundred and ten million, sixty thousand, two hundred thirty-three.
2. Three billion, eight million, seven hundred and eight thousand, four hundred sixty-three.

The 1960s is read "the nineteen sixties" or "the sixties." The 1950s is read "the nineteen fifties" or "the fifties."

1. How do you read these?
   1940s
   1930s
2. The seventies is written: 1970s
   The eighties is written: _____
   The twenties is written: _____

Bibliography

APFEL, Necia. *The Moon and Its Exploration.* New York: Franklin Watts, 1982.

ASIMOV, Isaac. *The Earth's Moon.* Milwaukee: G. Stevens, 1988.

BEAL, Merrill. *The Grand Canyon: The Story Behind the Scenery.* Flagstaff, Ariz.: K.C. Publications, 1968.

BERGER, Melvin. *Computers in Your Life.* New York: Thomas Crowell, 1981.

BRAMLY, Franklin. *Sun Dogs and Shooting Stars.* Boston: Houghton Mifflin, 1980.

BRAMLEY, Franklin. *The Moon Seems to Change.* New York: Crowell, 1987.

BRAMWELL, Martyn. *The Ocean.* New York: F. Watts, 1987.

BRINDZE, Ruth. *The Story of Our Calendar.* New York: Vanguard Press, 1949.

BUEHR, Walter. *Keeping Time.* New York: G.P. Putnam's Sons, 1960.

CALDICOTT, Helen. *Missile Envy: The Arms Race and Nuclear War.* New York: Bantam, 1986.

DIXON, Dougal. *Deserts and Wastelands.* New York: F. Watts, 1984.

DIXON, Dougal. *Geology.* New York: F. Watts, 1982.

DWIGGINS, Don. *Eagle Has Landed.* San Carlos, Calif.: Golden Gate Junior Books, 1970.

ESTERER, Arnulf. *Saying It Without Words: Signs and Symbols.* New York: Messner, 1980.

FARA, Patricia. *Computers—How They Work and What They Do.* London: Pelham Books, 1983.

GIBBONS, Gail. *Weather Forecasting.* New York: Four Winds Press, 1987.

GIRARD, Linda. *Earth, Sea and Sky: The Work of Edmund Halley.* Niles, Ill.: A. Whitman & Co., 1985.

GRAHAM, Ada. *The Changing Desert.* New York: Scribner, 1981.

KEHR, Ernest A. *My Hobby Is Collecting Stamps.* New York: Hart Book Co., 1955.

KNOWLTON, Jack. *Maps and Globes.* New York: Crowell, 1985.

MODLEY, Rudolf. *Handbook of Pictorial Symbols.* New York: Dover Publications, 1976.

MOODY, Ralph. *Riders of the Pony Express.* Boston: Houghton Mifflin, 1958.

PETTIGREW, Mark. *Planet Earth.* New York: Gloucester Press, 1987.

PETTIGREW, Mark. *Weather.* New York: Gloucester Press, 1987.

RICHARDSON, Joy. *What Happens When You Think?* Milwaukee: G. Stevens, 1986.

RUTLAND, Jonathan. *The Sea.* Morristown, N.J.: Silver Burdett & Co., 1983.

SHARP, Pat. *Brain Power.* New York: William Morrow Co., 1984.

SHUTTLESWORTH, Dorothy. *The Moon, Stepping Stone to Outer Space.* New York: Doubleday and Company, 1977.

SIMON, Seymour. *Meet the Computer.* New York: Crowell, 1985.

STAFFORD, Patricia. *Your Two Brains.* New York: Atheneum, 1986.

VIGNA, Judith. *Nobody Wants a Nuclear War.* Niles, Ill.: A. Whitman & Co., 1986.

WEISS, Ann. *The Nuclear Arms Race: Can We Survive It?* New York: Houghton Mifflin, 1983.

WHITE, Jack. *How Computers Really Work.* New York: Dodd, Mead, 1986.

ZWASS, Vladimir. *Introduction to Computer Science.* New York: Barnes & Noble Books, 1981.

CLARKE, M.A., and S. Silberstein. "Towards a Realization of Psycholinguistic Principles in the ESL Classroom." *Language Learning* 27(1): 135–54, 1977.

CLARKE, Mark. "The Short Circuit Hypothesis of ESL Reading or When Language Competence Interferes With Reading Performance." *Modern Language Journal* 64(2):203–9.

DEVINE, Joanne. "A Case Study of Two Readers: Models of Reading and Reading Performance." *Interactive Approaches to Teaching Reading,* edited by Patricia Carrell, Joanne Devine, & David Eskey. New York: Cambridge University Press, 1988.

ESKEY, David, and William Grabel. "Interactive Models for Second Language Reading: Perspectives on Instructions." *Interactive Approaches to Teaching Reading,* edited by Carrell, Devine, & Eskey. New York: Cambridge University Press, 1988.

GOODMAN, Kenneth. *Language and Literacy: The Selected Writings of Kenneth Goodman.* London: Routledge and Kegan Paul, 1975.

HUDSON, Thom. "Effects of Induced Schemata on the Short Circuit in L2 Reading: Non-decoding Factors in L2 Reading and Performance." *Language Learning* 32(1):3–31.

KOPFSTEIN, Robert W. "Fluent Reading, Language, and the Reading Teacher." *The Reading Teacher* 32, 1979.

KRASHEN, Stephen. "The Case for Narrow Reading." TESOL Newsletter 15(6), 1981.

RIGG, Pat. "The Miscue—ESL Project." *On TESOL 77: Teaching and Learning ESL: Trends in Research and Practice.* Washington, D.C.: TESOL, 1977.

SAMUELS, Jay. "The Method of Repeated Readings." *The Reading Teacher* 32(4):403–8, 1979.

Answers to Crossword Puzzle on page 90

Answers to Crossword Puzzle on page 184